T0358190

Cambridge Elements ≡

Elements in Applied Evolutionary Science
edited by
David F. Bjorklund
Florida Atlantic University

SUPERORGANISM

Toward a New Social Contract for Our Endangered Species

Peter A. Corning
Institute for the Study of Complex Systems

 THE EVOLUTION INSTITUTE

CAMBRIDGE
UNIVERSITY PRESS

CAMBRIDGE
UNIVERSITY PRESS

Shaftesbury Road, Cambridge CB2 8EA, United Kingdom

One Liberty Plaza, 20th Floor, New York, NY 10006, USA

477 Williamstown Road, Port Melbourne, VIC 3207, Australia

314–321, 3rd Floor, Plot 3, Splendor Forum, Jasola District Centre, New Delhi – 110025, India

103 Penang Road, #05–06/07, Visioncrest Commercial, Singapore 238467

Cambridge University Press is part of Cambridge University Press & Assessment, a department of the University of Cambridge.

We share the University's mission to contribute to society through the pursuit of education, learning and research at the highest international levels of excellence.

www.cambridge.org
Information on this title: www.cambridge.org/9781009400428
DOI: 10.1017/9781009400404

First published 2023

A catalogue record for this publication is available from the British Library.

ISBN 978-1-009-40042-8 Paperback
ISSN 2752-9428 (online)
ISSN 2752-941X (print)

Superorganism

Toward a New Social Contract for Our Endangered Species

Elements in Applied Evolutionary Science

DOI: 10.1017/9781009400404
First published online: May 2023

Peter A. Corning
Institute for the Study of Complex Systems
Author for correspondence: Peter A. Corning, pacorning@complexsystems.org

Abstract: As evidence of our global survival crisis continues to mount, the expression "too little, too late" comes to mind. We all live in an interdependent world which has an increasingly shared fate. We are participants in an emerging global "superorganism" that is dependent on close cooperation. Indeed, positive synergy (cooperative effects) has been the key to our evolutionary success as a species. However, our ultimate fate is now in jeopardy. Going forward, we must either create a more effective global society (with collective self-governance) or our species will very likely be convulsed by mass starvation, waves of desperate migrants, and lethal social conflict. The greatest threat we may face is each other, and a regression into tribalism and violent conflict. This Element has a more hopeful prescription for a new global social contract. It is based on the many examples of superorganisms – socially organized species – in the natural world, and in evolution.

Keywords: basic needs, global governance, equality, equity, social contract

ISBNs: 9781009400428 (PB), 9781009400404 (OC)
ISSNs: 2752-9428 (online), 2752-941X (print)

Contents

1 A Preview of the Near Future

Imagine this scenario. The megadrought that has gripped the southwestern part of the United States is now in its fifteenth year. Relentless global warming and a major climate change – what the climatologists call a "regime shift" – has guaranteed that there will be no reprieve in the foreseeable future. This drought could last for 50 or 100 years, or more. It has happened before.

Six western states, including California, Arizona, New Mexico, Nevada, Utah, and parts of Texas, along with a large swath of northern Mexico, have been devastated by the drought. Vital rivers, especially the Colorado, the Sacramento, and the San Joaquin, have all but dried up, and many of the underground aquifers in the region have been severely depleted. A crash effort to build water desalination plants along the coastlines of California and the Gulf of Mexico will take many years to complete. Most of the 5,300 dams that once provided water and hydroelectric power for the region have also gone dormant. Conversion to solar and wind power is an option only for those who can afford to pay for it. Governments everywhere are strapped for money.

Without water, electric power, or employment, entire cities in the region – from Phoenix to Las Vegas, El Paso, and the Los Angeles basin – have become near ghost towns, while many other cities are on life support. Raging wildfires have destroyed many of the region's forests. California's huge economy (once the sixth largest in the world) has also been decimated, and almost half the total regional population, about twenty-five million people, have been forced to evacuate. The adjacent states and western Canada have been flooded with climate refugees. Massive refugee camps, with tens of thousands of recreational vehicles (RVs), campers, trucks, tents, and people living in their cars have been set up by FEMA (the Federal Emergency Management Agency), with added support from the World Food Programme (WFP) and a broad array of private agencies. But with similar climate shifts occurring in several other parts of the world, from India to China, Russia, and North Africa, the relief agencies are all overwhelmed and running out of money. Severe shortages of food, water, sanitation, health care and other resources inside the refugee camps have resulted in widespread hunger, degenerating health, disease epidemics, frequent murders and suicides, rampant drug-taking, and a general loss of hope.

Meanwhile, global food prices have more than quintupled, especially for vital grains and legumes but also for meat, seafood, and vegetables of all kinds. Before the drought, California alone was producing about one-quarter of all the vegetables grown in the United States, as well as many fruits, grains, and livestock. With the war in Ukraine and simultaneous droughts occurring in several countries, food shortages have become a global crisis. As a result, world poverty, which was hovering at about 20–30 percent of the world population back in 2015 (World Bank, 2022a), has risen to nearly 50 percent. More than 100 million children go to sleep hungry every night. A loaf of bread, when you can find it (and can afford it), might cost $25. A gallon of bottled water could cost even more.

The drought has also dealt a severe blow to the global economic system. The long predicted "ultimate recession" has set in, and the downward slide has now surpassed the Great Depression in the 1930s. Before the drought, automation, robots, remote work, and self-driving cars and trucks had already taken a toll on employment. Now joblessness in industrialized countries has climbed to over 35 percent. Indeed, the fundamental drivers of the entire capitalist system – innovation, expanding markets and trade, increasing sales, rising revenues, and growing wealth – have all collapsed, along with stock portfolios, real estate values, and personal savings. Mortgage defaults have skyrocketed, and many banks have failed. A deep and debilitating poverty has set in. Several countries have already defaulted on their national debts.

Civil society has also degenerated in places that have been hardest hit. A particular flash point is the steady stream of water trucks and food trucks that are coming into the affected southwestern states in armed convoys to serve affluent families, businesses, and government officials. Many wealthy residents have simply moved out of the region, along with numerous businesses. The high-tech companies in Silicon Valley, for instance, have mostly relocated to Detroit and the Great Lakes region. Schools, colleges, libraries, professional sports, and many other institutions in the region are on lockdown or have been closed. Disneyland is history, a deserted, rusting relic. Food riots and other forms of mass protests have long since given way to anarchic vandalism and violence, and organized assaults by armed militia gangs, along with ruthless police-state repression, ever-expanding concentration camps, and a kind of every man for himself social philosophy.

Similar climate-driven convulsions have been occurring in other countries as well. China, for instance, has responded to desertification in the north and a series of floods along its two vital rivers and agricultural heartland with a wholesale military occupation of East Africa, greatly increasing the vast farming enclaves it already owned there. The daily parade of container ships with grains and vegetables destined to feed China's huge population (and its livestock) are being guarded from attack by pirates by an ascendant Chinese navy. Meanwhile Russia, suffering a prolonged drought in its prime agricultural provinces, has overrun and all but enslaved Ukraine, Eastern Europe, and the Baltic countries. A weakened, impoverished America, with a huge budget deficit, trillions of dollars of indebtedness toward an emboldened China, and intimidated by Russia's formidable nuclear arsenal, has not resisted these moves.

Now things are about to get even worse. A new dark age has begun, and hundreds of millions will die, along with the rule of law and all the trappings of civilization. The global life-support system that sustains us all is breaking down. Charles Darwin (1968/1859) characterized it as "the struggle for existence" – the survival of the fittest. Evolutionary biologists refer to it as an "extinction event."

This dark future scenario is, of course, only a projection, but the odds are that something along these lines (or even worse) will happen sooner rather than later if we remain on our present course as a divided and deeply competitive world of individual countries focused on their own narrow self-interests. The recent surge in polarizing nationalism and the rising tide of conflicts between various countries is an ominous development. The prolonged, destructive war in Ukraine is especially disturbing.

Despite recent efforts to mobilize global action, such as the 2022 United Nations (UN) biodiversity conference in Canada (COP15) and the 2022 COP27 climate conference in Egypt (where various voluntary commitments were made), our global civilization has failed, on the whole, to respond effectively to our ever-growing survival crisis. We are all participants in an emerging global "superorganism" that is dependent on close cooperation.[1] This has long been the key to our spectacular evolutionary success as a species. However, our ultimate fate is now in serious jeopardy. A hangman's noose is tightening around the collective neck of the human species. And it is a doomsday rope with several deadly strands.

One of these strands, quite obviously, is global warming and accelerating climate change. Climate warming is already causing lethal mischief to the environment and to our species in various ways. Droughts, floods, tsunamis, and hurricanes, for instance, are age-old threats, but they have become bigger and more frequent. Killer heat waves are having a devastating effect on our food production and rampant wildfires are consuming our vital forests. A recent report from the UN Intergovernmental Panel on Climate Change (IPCC),

---

[1] In an article on the emerging global superorganism as a cybernetic system, Francis Heylighen (2007), the well-known cybernetic theorist, stressed the role of information technology in addition to increased cooperation via a division of labor. While I agree with the importance of these factors, I side with the biologists Bert Hölldobler and Edward O. Wilson (2009) in their masterful textbook on the insect societies, *The Superorganism*, where they show that the term refers, most importantly, to "a collective survival enterprise" not to structural (cybernetic) analogies with organisms as living systems. Indeed, insect societies come in various forms, but the common denominator in every case is that they represent collective "units" of selection for survival and reproduction. This, I believe, is more consistent with the original meaning of the term.

warned that we have less than a decade to make drastic reductions in our greenhouse gas emissions, and the response to date has been nothing short of alarming (Flavelle, 2019; Lu & Flavelle, 2019). An updated IPCC report, issued in 2023, warns that the world will most likely miss the critical climate-warming target of limiting the increase to less than 1.5 degrees Celsius (2.7 degrees Fahrenheit) within the current decade. A failure to do so will have catastrophic consequences, the report concludes (Boehm & Schumer, 2023).

Another major threat is a global food system that is already seriously eroding – with declining topsoil, severely depleted irrigation water supplies, and shrinking fisheries, among other things. Even now, perhaps 30 percent of the world's population is not properly fed (FAO, 2021) (the estimates vary with up to as many as one billion people being affected). This too is going to get much worse, along with growing shortages of fresh water and an increasing potential for water wars between neighboring countries. Our global freshwater challenges are detailed in another recent UN report (United Nations, 2022)

A third major threat is our relentlessly increasing global population, now at eight billion people and projected to grow to an estimated eleven billion by 2100, an increase of 38 percent. If unchecked, this trend is destined to become a self-inflicted Malthusian disaster. It was the Reverend Thomas Malthus (2008/ 1798) who first predicted the dire consequences of unrestrained population growth: "Hunger and poverty, vice and crime, pestilence and famine, revolution and war."

All this says nothing about rising sea levels, where the worst-case scenarios predict that many of the world's major cities may be under water – or become sea-walled fortresses – well before the end of this century. Many – like Venice in 2019 – are already having serious flooding problems (Phelan, 2022).

Then there is our capitalist economic system, with ever-increasing extremes of concentrated wealth at the very top and widespread poverty among the rest of the population. With some notable exceptions (see Section 5), the world's economies are falling short, or even failing, in their primary obligation to provide for the basic needs of their citizens. Add to this the current gridlock of governmental dysfunction, endemic corruption, failed states, self-serving authoritarian leaders, renewed big power rivalries, and, not least, a polarized and increasingly angry global population that is awash with destructive weapons. And this is only the short list. The liberal, democratic world order that was created after World War Two seems to be unraveling, and the threat of virulent nationalism and lethal global conflict seems to be growing. (Corning, 2018; see also, Chayes, 2015).

The image of a rope with many strands happens to be a classic example of synergy – a whole that is greater than the sum of its parts – and it was first used by Ecclesiastes in the Old Testament. However, our metaphorical twenty-first-century rope is a horrendous example of negative synergy, a darkly menacing nexus that is much worse than any of its parts. Call it Malthus on steroids.

We still have a chance to make a bold positive choice going forward. But we must seize the opportunity that still exists to create a sustainable global society based on cooperation and mutually beneficial interdependence – a global super-organism. Positive synergy is the key, for it has always been the driver of our evolution as a species. But this, in turn, will require the replacement of an individualistic, competitive (nationalistic) social ethic with new social and political values – and a sublimation of our global economic system to the ancient principle of the "common good." In other words, we must reverse the ominous current trend toward increased division and conflict in world politics and economics.

We now know that the rise of complex living organisms over the past 3.9 billion years has been driven by cooperation and synergies – not zero-sum competition. From the very origins of life to the emergence of socially organized species such as honeybees, meerkats, mole rats, leaf-cutter ants, and (of course) humankind, close cooperation, innovation, and synergies of various kinds – mutual benefits that are not otherwise attainable – have played a key role. I call it "nature's magic" (see Corning, 1983, 2003, 2005; Hölldobler & Wilson, 2009).

In humankind, our immensely complex division of labor – or what should properly be called a "combination of labor" – has exerted a powerful influence in determining our extraordinary success as a species. Because an organized society is much like a living organism, with many specialized parts that depend on each other and on the success of the "whole" – an analogy that goes back to the ancient Greek philosopher Plato (1946/380 BC) in his classic study *The Republic* – modern-day biologists commonly use the term "superorganism" to characterize this special kind of organized social interdependence (Hölldobler & Wilson, 2009). We must now take this cooperative strategy to the next level and create a sustainable *global* superorganism – or else. We must think outside the box because the future lies outside the box.

In this Element I will briefly review the growing evidence for our impending life-and-death crisis as a species. To repeat, there is much more involved than global warming, although climate change is our single greatest threat. I will draw attention to the tightening hangman's noose (as many others have done in recent years) in the belief that the fate of our species is truly at stake. We face a collective choice like none other in our long, multi-million-year history (and prehistory) as a ground-dwelling bipedal ape. Will we act for the common good as a species or will we descend into a "war of each against all" (or each nation against all) as the philosopher Thomas Hobbes (2010/1651) famously warned us long ago? Will the future be about serving the needs of all of "us" collectively, or will it be about a mutually destructive clash between "us" and "them"? This is our fundamental choice (see Corning, 2018; also see Bremmer, 2018).

Perverse as it may seem, the greatest threat we may face is each other – and a regression into tribalism and violent conflict. Indeed, collective violence has been one of the major themes in human history, going as far back in time as the evidence allows us to go (Corning, 2018). It has long been a part of our problem-solving "toolkit" as a species. We now face the very real prospect of an era of global violence and "climate wars." Or worse. Perhaps most ominous is the rise of authoritarianism and especially the growing signs of conflict between the democratic West and authoritarian regimes (most notably China and Russia), which could override our shared interests (see especially Applebaum, 2020).

Equally important, the challenges we face going forward will very often transcend national borders – from megadroughts to lethal disease epidemics and the hordes of climate refugees. One estimate from the World Bank (2022b) predicts it could reach 216 million. Another estimate, from UN Secretary-General Antonio Guterres (2023), puts the eventual refugee total from low-lying coastal areas at close to 900 million. Even more disturbing is an environmental model developed by a global team of researchers (Chaplin-Kramer et al., 2019) which projects that, within the next thirty years, the number of people without sufficient food and water could number in the billions. These unprecedented life-and-death challenges will overwhelm the ability of most countries to deal with them unaided. They will pose unimaginable humanitarian, security, and military threats.

We have two paths available to us going forward. We must either create a more effective global superorganism (with collective governance) or else our species will very likely be convulsed by mass starvation, waves of desperate migrants, lethal social conflict, and perhaps even devolve and go all but extinct. There is, I will argue, no standpat, status quo option.

In this Element, I will also explore some of the potential consequences of these alternatives – for ourselves, for our children, and for our species. As I will propose, only an organized process of major social, economic, and political change on a global scale offers us genuine reason for long-term hope. It would be transformative for our species, and it would be unprecedented in the history of life on Earth. Our species is already unique in many ways, but now we need to take the next step. I believe this option is like a powerful magnetic field that will draw us in if we can find our compasses and get them properly aligned. That is the goal of this Element. I will outline a master plan and roadmap for a new, more legitimate and sustainable economic and political world order – a global social contract and a global superorganism.

Walter Lippmann, one of the great political commentators of the twentieth century, warned us about our overarching governance problem in a 1969 interview shortly before he died (Brandon, 1969). His words, more than ever, ring true.

> This is not the first time that human affairs have been chaotic and seemed ungovernable. But never before, I think, have the stakes been so high ... What is really pressing upon us is that the need to be governed ... threatens to exceed man's capacity to govern ... The supreme question before mankind – to which I shall not live to know the answer – is how men will be able to make themselves willing and able to save themselves.

A half century later, we still do not know the answer to Lippmann's "supreme question." However, I believe we do have a path forward. It leads to a new social contract and an effective global superorganism that can act on behalf of the public trust. Now we must find the collective will to choose this path, because the future is already underway.[2]

2 "The Future Is Not What It Used to Be"

Astronomers and astrophysicists use the term "singularity" to describe a unique celestial event, like the "Big Bang" or a black hole (though we now know that black holes are quite common). These days the term singularity is also being used to characterize the potential consequences of artificial intelligence and robotics. The claim is that transformative economic and social changes might result from adopting these leading-edge technologies. One expert estimate puts the ultimate number of job losses at 400–800 million (McKinsey Global Institute, 2017). Other estimates are even higher.

I am hardly alone in believing that we are in fact facing another, much greater singularity, one that will swamp the futuristic visions of the technophiles. It may even be life-threatening for our entire species. Our planet could literally become uninhabitable for humans.

Over the past 12,000 years, during what geologists call the Holocene Epoch, the global climate has been unusually stable and benign, despite many local weather traumas at various times – droughts, floods, deep freezes, etc. This magic window of relative climate stability is referred to as an "interglacial." Before the Holocene interglacial, our evolving ancestors had to cope with a climate and environment that was wildly variable. The evidence shows that

---

[2] Some of the material in this volume was also used in my introductory chapter, "Teleonomy in evolution: 'The ghost in the machine'," in *Evolution "On Purpose": Teleonomy in Living Systems*, edited by P. A. Corning, S. A, Kauffman, D. Noble, J. A. Shapiro, R. Vane-Wright, and A. Pross (MIT Press, 2023).

there have been some twenty-seven ice ages over the past 3.5 million years alone, and that many of these climate shifts involved rapid, drastic changes in landforms and local environments across the world. For instance, during the ice age that began about 33,000 years ago and peaked around 13,000 years later, sea levels declined more than 400 feet from their present levels, as a mile-high mountain of ice became trapped in the northern glaciers. Then the process went into reverse (see my book, *Synergistic Selection: How Cooperation Has Shaped Evolution and the Rise of Humankind* [Corning, 2018]; see also Cochran & Harpending, 2009).

Our remote ancestors were able to cope with these radical changes because their groups were small; they were highly mobile and adaptable; they were opportunistic hunter-gatherer bands that relied on native plant foods and the huge herds of migrating meat-on-the-hoof (as well as plentiful sources of seafood); and they could pick up and move on if the local environment turned hostile. There was ample room to adapt, and even to expand their numbers over time.

It is not coincidental that the rise of agriculture and complex urban societies, along with the explosive growth of the human population from perhaps a - few million to almost eight billion today and still increasing, coincided with the Holocene interglacial. Our modern agricultural and animal husbandry systems absolutely depend on a stable, moderate environment with fertile topsoil and lots of fresh water. And so do we.

Now the human species is crowded into every inhabitable niche. We are all tied to strictly bounded (though often contested) territories and to fixed food production systems. We can no longer simply move on without becoming refugees or making war on our neighbors, much less find unexploited new sources of food and water. We cannot turn back. However, our resource base as a species, and our ability to provide the wherewithal for meeting our basic survival needs, has become seriously overstretched and unstable. There are many alarming signs of severe stress in our natural environment. Ecologists refer to it as an "overshoot" (one study concluded that our "ecological over-shoot" [across more than 140 countries] has exceeded sustainable yields by more than 50 percent, overall, and is getting worse; Fanning et al., 2022). We confront a convergence of self-made crises. Call it a "perfect storm," a "tipping point," a "punctuated equilibrium," an "inflection point," or, more precisely, a potential catastrophe.

We are losing control and are faced with a collective choice that will have long-term evolutionary consequences. If we do not make a concerted, global, and (most important) cooperative change in our basic survival strategy as a species we will almost certainly unleash unimaginable destructive forces.

The wry and perceptive observation that "the future is not what it used to be," which dates back to the late 1930s in the shadow of World War Two, has now become an even darker and more ominous warning.

The naysayers, deniers, and belittlers of this unabashedly alarmist scenario have been plentiful. Optimists like Steven Pinker (2018), in his best-selling book *Enlightenment Now: The Case for Reason, Science, Humanism, and Progress*, point to how much better off so many of us are than we were even 100 years ago. He sees a bright future ahead. And Yuval Noah Harari (2017), in his popular book *Homo Deus: A Brief History of Tomorrow*, assures us that we have managed to "rein in" the Malthusian scourges of famines, plagues, and wars. They are now "manageable challenges," he says.

For these and other techno-futurists, progress is still an article of faith. They scoff at what they see as defeatist views. They point to the myriad of ways in which we are already responding to our challenges, from the 2015 Paris Climate Accord and the various follow-up meetings (like COP15 and COP27 in 2022) to the rapidly growing percentage of renewable solar and wind power worldwide and the emerging market for electric cars and trucks. Many others are trying to consume less and recycle more. Or plant more trees. But this is much too little, and it could very soon be too late. Consider just some of the deeply disturbing indicators:

- **The consequences of global warming:** CO_2 levels in the atmosphere have now crossed 415 parts per million, more than double the levels measured in the nineteenth century and getting close to the limit of 450 parts per million set by climate scientists in 2015 as an absolute ceiling to prevent a calamity. Seventeen of the past eighteen years have been the hottest on record, 2 degrees Fahrenheit higher on average than at the start of the nineteenth century. If this trend continues, there will be major long-term climate shifts. The disappearance of mountain glaciers and winter snowpacks, a process already well underway, will drastically reduce vital river-water runoff and with it the water resources that two-thirds of the human species depend on for survival. Especially alarming is the loss of glaciers in the Himalayas and Tibet, which feed many of Asia's major rivers. Heat waves will also decimate livestock and our fragile vegetable and grain crops. For instance, the months-long heat wave in western Russia in 2010 destroyed 40 percent of that country's grain crops and led to a temporary tripling of world grain prices. Several European countries also suffered serious crop losses during the prolonged summer heat wave/drought in 2018. This was also the year when Cape Town, South Africa nearly ran out of fresh water. (See Pierre-Louis, 2018.)

And that's not all. Our complex agricultural systems are also very vulnerable, with many moving parts. One study by a team of researchers in 2017 found that for every degree Celsius above the nominal average growing temperature there would be a decline in yields of wheat (6%), rice (3.2%), corn (7.2%), and soybeans (3.1%) (Chuang & Bing, 2017). Another study, in India, found that a 2 degree Celsius increase reduced wheat yields in different locations by 37–58 percent (Brown, 2009; Guram, 2022). Especially troubling is the recent discovery that increasing atmospheric CO_2 levels are reducing the nutritional value of rice, the main staple food for two billion people. More frequent and destructive droughts, storms, heat waves, and wildfires – a trend already well advanced – will also disrupt food production in many ways and cause many trillions of dollars in damage over time. Ocean warming and acidification (not to mention the effects of pollution) will severely harm an ocean food chain that is already under severe stress; it could threaten close to 20 percent of humankind's food supply. (Recent data suggests that the oceans are warming 40 percent faster than in the 1980s.) Most of the world's fisheries have already maxed out and some are in steep decline.

In sum, global warming is a major threat to our food production systems, and to the survival of our species. A 2014 prediction by the IPCC of a 2–6 percent decline in global crop yields every decade going forward seems now to be too conservative. If the trend continues, it could very soon cause chaos in the world food economy, and in our politics. Of course, extreme heat can also kill people. A recent World Bank (2022a) report concluded that some 800 million people in South Asia, especially in large cities, are dangerously at risk from summer heat waves. If we continue on the same path in terms of global warming, the world will be 5–10 degrees Fahrenheit hotter on average by 2100 and the Arctic an alarming 15 degrees Fahrenheit hotter. There will soon be many tens of millions of desperate climate refugees. (See Markham, 2018.)

- **Shrinking freshwater resources:** Some 70 percent of our freshwater usage is for irrigating crops, and another 10 percent is for domestic purposes, but we are running a serious global deficit in the rate of water consumption. Most disturbing is the rapid drawdown of underground aquifers around the world. Some of them can be recharged over time, but many others cannot. According to a recent study (Dalin et al., 2017), at least fifteen major countries with half the world's population – including the United States, China, India, Pakistan, Iran, Mexico, and several Middle Eastern countries – are running large water deficits. Their water tables are rapidly declining. Another recent study by NASA, using satellite data, indicated that twenty-one of the world's thirty-seven largest aquifers are seriously depleted (Milius, 2017). For instance, the huge Ogallala aquifer, which spans portions of eight states in the American southwest and provides irrigation water for some 27 percent of US farm products, is expected to be depleted within fifty years (Leahy, 2019; Griggs et al., 2020). Even more alarming is a new government report in India, which concluded that some 600 million of its people even now face extreme water scarcity, and that 200,000 people a year are dying from unsafe or insufficient water (Abi-Habib & Kumar, 2018). By 2030, the report warned, that country's total demand could be twice the available supply.

Many of the world's vital rivers – the Yellow, Nile, Indus, Colorado, Tigris, Euphrates, Mekong, and Jordan among others – are also depleted and the level of grain production along their fertile river deltas has been reduced. China, India, Egypt, Iran, Mexico, and other countries that were once self-sufficient in grains are now large-scale importers. Likewise, many of the world's freshwater lakes have been heavily overused and some have dried up completely – from Lake Chad in Africa to Owens Lake in California. China, an extreme example, has lost more than half of its 4,000 lakes. The continued overuse and drawdown (and pollution) of vital freshwater resources in various countries guarantees a future of severe food and water shortages – and increased political conflict. Among the powder kegs for future water wars are the major rivers that span national boundaries.

- **Topsoil depletion:** A 2022 UN report estimated that fully 90 percent of the Earth's topsoil is likely to be at risk by 2050 (FAO, 2022). There are many causes – deforestation, soil erosion, dust storms, salt buildup in irrigated soils, overuse of agricultural pesticides and other chemicals, droughts, overgrazing of grasslands, and the conversion of farmland to housing and commercial uses. (Once upon a time, Silicon Valley was a picturesque region of farms and orchards known locally as "The Valley of the Heart's Delight." Alas, that world is long gone.) Even in areas where topsoil is not severely depleted, the productivity of the soil is being undermined in many cases by modern agricultural practices that destroy vital organisms – symbiotic bacteria, mycorrhizal fungi, and the all-important beneficial earth worms. As President Franklin Roosevelt put it in a 1937 speech, "A nation that destroys its soils destroys itself."

- **Rising sea levels:** The combination of ocean warming and melting ice caps, resulting in an (accelerating) 8-inch sea-level rise over the past century, is already causing major problems. In the United States, for example, Miami, Charleston, and Norfolk are already having to cope with significant flooding during "king tides." Higher sea levels have also exacerbated storm surges in some of the recent hurricanes, from Katrina to Sandy. New data indicate that the Antarctic ice sheet is now melting six times faster than in the 1980s, while the Greenland ice sheet may be close to a "tipping point" for a catastrophic decline (Boers & Rypdal, 2021). If this trend should continue, an 8-foot sea-level rise is the low estimate.

Longer term, the projections for sea-level rise are as high as 23 feet. And this is not even the worst case. In the remote past, when there were no polar ice caps and all the Earth was tropical, sea levels were 80 feet higher. Two-thirds of the world's cities and close to half of the global population are only a few feet above existing sea levels. We will have three choices going forward: suffer the consequences, mitigate the problem with sea walls and other retaining technologies, or else evacuate. Long term, only the latter option will remain (evacuation), and the economic, social, and political impacts will be convulsive, even catastrophic. (See Mooney, 2019.)

- **"The Population Bomb":** Biologist Paul Ehrlich (1968) was much praised but later much criticized for his best-selling (now legendary) book carrying the famous title *The Population Bomb.* He concluded: "The battle to feed all of humanity is over. In the 1970s hundreds of millions of people will starve to death, despite any crash programs embarked upon now" Ehrlich (1968: xi). In retrospect, Ehrlich was only a bit off in his timing. He could not anticipate the temporary gains achieved by the so-called Green Revolution. The battle to feed humanity continues, but we are still losing the war. As the global population continues to grow – with perhaps two to three billion more mouths to feed by 2050 – our capacity to meet the increase in demand is foundering. A recent UN study estimated that, in order to provide adequate nutrition for the world's projected population in 2050, including the estimated 800 million to 1 billion who are currently undernourished or malnourished, a 56 percent increase in food production will be necessary (World Resources Institute, 2019). Despite the recent surge in agricultural innovation and entrepreneurial ventures, this probably will not happen. What will happen instead is what Malthus (and Ehrlich) predicted (see also Ehrlich & Ehrlich, 2012; Ehrlich & Harte, 2015).

- **The economic inequality "bomb":** This is also a major threat to our future as a species. Although there is an issue of fairness and social justice involved, what threatens us most is the economic consequences of poverty for the great mass of "have-nots." The concentration of income and wealth among the top 10 percent globally (much of it in the top 1 percent) means that many of the estimated 15 to 30 percent of us who are living in poverty (depending on which measuring rod is used) do not have the "discretionary income" or the savings needed to cope with the coming scarcities and inevitable sharp increases in the cost of food, water, energy, housing, and other necessities. It is the poor, predominately, who will be caught in the Malthusian trap. (A recent survey found that fewer than half of Americans have even $1,000 saved up for emergencies and 32 percent have nothing at all [Gillespie, 2023].) Economic inflation is how the middle class becomes poor, and how the poor starve to death. And history shows that the victims are unlikely to go quietly into this oblivion. (More on this in Section 3.)

- **"Us" versus "them" and the tribalism trap:** Human psychology and our deep history as a species poses another serious obstacle to dealing with our global survival challenge and creates a huge threat to our collective future. Both ancient wisdom and modern science (not to mention the historical record and the news media) confirm that humankind has a built-in behavioral predisposition to form close-knit cooperative groups, while, at the same time, reacting with suspicion and hostility to strangers, outsiders, and members of other groups, especially when threatened. Our species evolved over several million years in small, interdependent hunter-gatherer bands that had to compete (for the most part) against other bands, as well as other species. Sometimes our remote ancestors cooperated with their neighbors and developed trading relationships, but more often they were lethal adversaries. "Warfare" between hominin groups was common, and this heritage has shaped our social psychology. We are at once capable of sacrificing our lives for members of our own group while slaughtering "enemies" without remorse. The technical terms for this bipolar behavior pattern are "ethnocentrism" and "xenophobia." It's often referred to, in both scientific and popular literature, as "we vs. they," or "us vs. them." (Some of the underlying neurobiology and biochemistry is also now well understood.)

We can see this polarizing dynamic at work in such intractable social problems as racism, religious discrimination, conflicts between economic groups, partisan politics, the recent alarming surge of nationalism, and, of course, in organized revolutions and warfare. It is also a ubiquitous part of our daily lives; every social group and organization has its "insiders" and "outsiders." Most important, the "we vs. they" syndrome undergirds the division of our species into some 195 independent countries that generally act in their own self-interest and frequently compete with other countries – or even make war with them. In the 1980s, at the end of the Cold War, it was hoped that a cooperative community of democratic nations might emerge from the ongoing process of economic and social globalization during the twentieth century. However, the recent resurgence of nationalist rivalries and harsh authoritarianism – not to mention civil wars in various countries and the war in Ukraine – has dashed this dream, and the proliferation of nuclear and biological weapons, plus international terrorism and cyberwarfare, makes the threat of a global conflagration very real. (See also Bremmer, 2018; Haberman, 2018.)

The future is not what it used to be! Indeed, economic collapse, rising political violence, and a problematic future for our species are very real possibilities, as many others have recently warned. Some have even given up hope. We are living in a uniquely dangerous time for the human species, and almost everyone is vulnerable in different ways. We are all susceptible to the devastating impact of climate change, from the grass huts of Pacific islanders to the "low bank" waterfront homes of wealthy Americans. Extreme weather events, it seems, can strike anywhere, anytime – as we have recently seen. And these traumatic events are becoming more violent, prolonged, and life-threatening. National borders no longer provide the security they once did in this new age of economic interdependence, international terrorism, cyberwarfare, wholesale migrations, lethal pandemics, and doomsday weapons that can be hurled over thousands of miles. (This is a crucially important point.)

The global food system is also increasingly interdependent, which means we are all affected by disruptions in food production in other countries. A decline in crop yields in, say, China may require everyone in the developed countries to pay much higher prices for their food. In addition to the menace of major droughts (the recent drought in India affected an estimated 320 million of its people), many countries have seen a trend in recent years toward declining crop yields, for a variety of reasons, even as the population has continued to increase. For instance, the ambitious wheat production program that Saudi Arabia initiated in the 1970s, based on tapping a large underground aquifer, increased yields by some three million tons annually but then had to be drastically scaled back and terminated as the aquifer was depleted. Other countries, such as Egypt and China, suffered reduced crop yields when they dammed major rivers and diverted some of the water from agriculture to other purposes. Fresh water pollution and contamination is also a major threat. The shortages caused by the war in Ukraine is just another example.

When economies are growing, social cooperation (and social harmony) depend on providing everyone with a fair share of the expanding economic pie. Unfortunately, this has not been happening in America and some other capitalist countries in recent decades, and it has led to an increase in internal social conflict. This is bad enough, but when the pie is shrinking, there is always a fateful choice to be made – who wins and who loses? Will the scarcities be rationed and shared for the "common good" (or, better said, the common bad), or will the self-interests of the rich and powerful – and the most powerful nations – ultimately prevail? This, in a nutshell, is the defining choice that we now face as individuals, as nations, and as a global society.

It has been said that we are living in an "end-time." It is a theme with many variations. First there was *The End of History* – political scientist Francis Fukuyama's (1992) optimistic prediction in the 1990s that the end of the Cold War would result in the ideological conflicts between nations being dissolved and the creation of a universal democratic, liberal world political order. This vision certainly did not end well. Then there was economist Jeffrey Sachs' (2006) hopeful recipe in his important book in which he envisioned *The End of Poverty*. This idea is not doing so well either. After the 2008–9 financial meltdown and the Great Recession, we had a glut of books predicting the end of economic growth and the end of capitalism, coupled with various dark economic forecasts and scenarios (see, for example, Streeck, 2016; Stiglitz, 2019). Over the past decade, it has seemed that capitalism has been thriving once again, along with nearly full employment in some countries – at least until the pandemic struck in 2020, followed by the war in Ukraine.

Our environmental crisis has become the latest "end-time" theme, but this one is very different. It is undergirded by a massive, multidisciplinary research enterprise and a mountain of evidence that goes back more than fifty years. I taught courses on the subject at Stanford University in the 1970s and 1980s. Many scientists have devoted their lives to it, and there are literally thousands of books and tens of thousands of scientific articles devoted to the problem. There have also been numerous political initiatives over the years that were thwarted by organized and well-financed opposition, as chronicled in depth by the journalist Nathaniel Rich (2019) in his book *Losing Earth*.

As the human future becomes ever-more precarious and the potential consequences seem ever-more catastrophic, the end-time warnings have become more apocalyptic and shrill, ranging from climate scientist James Hansen's (2009) authoritative *Storms of My Grandchildren*, to Peter Frase's (2016) *Four Futures* (including one scenario that foresees genocidal wars by the rich against the poor), John Michael Greer's (2016) *Dark Age America*, David Fleming's (2016) *Surviving the Future*, Jeff Nesbit's (2018) *This is the Way the World Ends*, David Wallace-Wells' (2019) *The Uninhabitable Earth*, and Bill McKibbon's (2019) *Falter*. Even the leading environmentalist and climate change expert, Lester Brown, has become alarmed. In his book, *World on the Edge: How to Prevent Environmental and Economic Collapse*, Brown (2011: 7) concludes: "Environmentally, the world is in overshoot mode . . . the environmental decline that will lead to economic decline and social collapse is well underway."

It is very late, but it is not yet too late for a "Plan B" (to borrow the term from Lester Brown's climate change recipe [see Brown, 2009, 2011]). We still have an opportunity to make a positive collective choice. In fact, we cannot avoid making a choice, even if we should choose not to choose and instead bury our collective heads in the quicksand. Call it denial, rejection, distraction, indifference, delusion, or perhaps even cynical self-interest. No one can predict exactly how the future will play out, but the danger is very real. And if we fail to make a positive collective choice, we will surrender our ability to exert control over the future and the destructive forces that will inevitably be unleashed. Unless we have a clear strategy and a set of guiding values, our responses are likely to be reactive, ad hoc, partisan, controversial, and almost certainly too little, too late.

In the simplest terms, we have two basic options going forward, each with far-reaching consequences, and neither one comes with a money-back guarantee. One option could be called the "common good" strategy. It would involve a collective commitment to work together and share the responsibility for making the necessary changes, along with a global effort to guarantee the basic needs of everyone in return for appropriate reciprocities. I call it the Fair Society model (Corning, 2011). A fair society must be the ethical foundation for a sustainable global superorganism. I believe it is our only hope for long-term global stability. (I will have much more to say about this in Section 6.)

The other option could be called the "survival of the fittest" strategy. It would preserve the existing global structure of wealth and power, and our (largely) unimpeded capitalist market system, along with the existing system of independent, often conflicting nation-states. To repeat, this option is oriented to the survival of the richest and most powerful – and the biggest and most powerful nations. Of course, this is the path we are already following, and it is a path that could lead us into a veritable snake pit of violent conflict. So, if we should choose not to choose, this is what we are likely to get.

Many of the "have-mores" (to borrow a line from former American President George Bush) are likely to prefer this option. That is probably a classic understatement. But if they (and we) deliberately choose to stay on the current path, all of us should consider the likely consequences, especially those that are unintended and uncontrollable. We should at least make an informed collective decision. This is what I will consider in more detail in the next section.

3 The Lessons of History: Past, Present, and Future

When the biophysicist Jeff Gore and a team of scientists at Massachusetts Institute of Technology (MIT) placed a colony of soil bacteria in a container along with an abundance of glucose and other nutrients, the colony grew exponentially at first but then went into a death spiral and crashed. The bacteria were poisoned by their own ever-increasing wastes and were rendered helpless to avoid the lethal consequences. Very evocative, needless to say!

Something quite different but equally catastrophic occurred in 1944 when the US Coast Guard introduced twenty-nine reindeer onto St. Matthew Island in the Bering Sea, where the vegetation was then abundant. However, there were also no major predators on the island. (Diamond, 2005). So, in the absence of any constraint, the herd grew to 6,000 animals by 1963, and, in the process, decimated their food supply. The end result was starvation and a population crash. By 1966, only forty-two reindeer were left, and by 1980 they were all gone. Once again, it was very evocative.

Or consider this iconic human example. The remote Easter Island in the south Pacific, long famous for its hundreds of massive stone statues, has also become a metaphor for a self-inflicted ecological disaster. Starting with a handful of Polynesian settlers in about 900 AD, the Easter Island population expanded over time to an estimated 20,000–30,000 people on an island that is only nine miles wide (about forty-four square miles). As their numbers grew, the islanders denuded the island's once thick forest, depleted its topsoil, wiped out its resident species of large birds, totally consumed a wood supply that was needed to build canoes for offshore fishing, and devolved into a dozen warring clans that suffered widespread starvation and even cannibalism. After the island's population had declined by an estimated 70 percent, a smallpox epidemic, unwittingly introduced by European traders, provided the coup de grace, along with the kidnapping of the island's remaining young men to become slave laborers.

The full story of Easter Island is complicated. Among other things, it involved a unique natural environment that was easily damaged and was unusually challenging for agriculture. However, the combination of wasteful and destructive social practices and uncontrolled population growth also played a major role. In his landmark book, *Collapse: How Societies Choose to Fail or Succeed*, Jared Diamond (2005: 118) concluded that "Easter's isolation makes it the clearest example of a [human] society that destroyed itself by overexploiting its own resources ... The parallels between Easter Island and the whole world are chillingly obvious."

The ecologists call it "eco-suicide," and it is far easier to do and more predictable than we had once thought. Indeed, our entire history as a species provides a cautionary tale. The archaeological record is littered with examples of ancient human societies that have vanished – many of them as victims of ecological disasters – from the very first city, Ur, to the Sumerians, Babylonians, Akkadians, Old Kingdom Egypt, the Hittites, Minoans, Mayans, Incas, Aztecs, Olmecs, Teotihuacan, the Anasazi, the Carthaginians, the Khmer Empire, and others.

Drawing on the case studies in his definitive study, Jared Diamond (2005) developed a five-point framework of causal factors that singly, or in combination, can lead to a societal collapse. These factors are: (1) environmental damage, (2) climate change, (3) the actions of hostile neighbors, (4) the loss (or lack) of friendly trading partners, and, most important, (5) how a society responds to its environmental constraints and emerging problems. Cultural values, social institutions, and the actions of leaders can make a huge difference to the outcome. For instance, Diamond pointed to examples of societies such as

Japan and the New Guinea Highlands that were able to avoid the fate of Easter Island by developing successful forest management practices (stick a pin in this point).

All of us today are living in a world where population growth and resource consumption have outstripped what the ecologists call our "carrying capacity." Our wastes, especially CO_2, have become a major threat. Nonrenewable resources are being rapidly depleted. Food shortages are becoming ever-more severe, and many nations are already scrambling for scarce food and water. There is, in fact, an emerging global competition for food and water resources that carries with it the potential to evoke mass violence (see Nolan et al., 2018).

Another flashpoint may be the various land (and water) acquisitions across national borders, either through outright purchases or long-term leases. These have multiplied in recent years. China, India, Egypt, South Korea, and Saudi Arabia are among the leaders in pursuing this acquisition strategy. It is ominous that many of these foreign acquisitions are being made through corrupt officials in poor countries that are struggling to feed their own people. Even the United States has become a target; foreign investors now own some thirty million acres of prime American farmland.

A third potential flashpoint for political conflict is the growing number of cases where governments have overruled the private sector and restricted the export of food products during a bad growing season. It seems that national self-interest can trump contractual obligations. The United States did it during the 1970s; Russia and Argentina did it with wheat in 2007; Vietnam did it that same year with rice; and Russia did it again during the great heat wave of 2010. Scarcity, by its very nature, converts cooperation into a zero-sum game – a game of winners and losers with, quite possibly, life-and-death consequences. Malthus meets game theory.

The philosopher George Santayana long ago warned us that "those who cannot remember the past are condemned to relive it," while Mark Twain is reputed to have said that history doesn't exactly repeat itself, but it does tend to rhyme. Indeed, it may even plagiarize itself. If we ignore the lessons of history, or else delude ourselves by thinking that the past is not relevant, our species will pay a terrible price.

To put it very simply, food and water scarcity breeds desperation, and desperation breeds resistance and revolt, and revolts are typically bloody and often end badly for everyone concerned. Bread – or the lack of it – was the underlying cause of the French Revolution in the eighteenth century and of the Russian and Chinese Revolutions in the twentieth century. In each case, the ruling classes resisted making changes and ultimately went to the guillotine, or to Siberian Gulags, or Chinese labor camps. Or to the death camps. Hitler came to power in the 1930s in a German nation that had been impoverished by punitive war reparations after its defeat in World War One and was then struck with runaway inflation and a deep economic recession.

Likewise, in the twenty-first century, the Arab Spring, the rise of ISIS terrorism, and the tragic civil war in Syria were almost certainly all triggered by a huge spike in grain prices and spreading hunger as a result of droughts in Syria, Russia, and elsewhere in the Middle East, combined with the diversion of a major share of America's corn crop into making ethanol fuel for automobiles and financial speculation in global commodity markets. The civil war in Yemen was presaged by severe water shortages and repeated dire warnings that were never heeded. And the "caravans" of refugees that have come from Central America to the southern border of the United States in the past few years were motivated by climate change and the dire consequences for agriculture in that region.

Thus, one of the great lessons of history (and prehistory) is that societies and their leaders (and their elites) often have fateful, life-and-death political choices to make, and these can play a decisive role in how a society responds to its challenges – as Jared Diamond (2019) has highlighted (see also Flannery & Marcus, 2012).

Consider the French Revolution. As in most other great political upheavals, there were a variety of factors that contributed to it. However, the common denominator – as in every other major revolution – was extreme poverty and hunger coupled with corruption and obscene wealth for the few, and a failure of the regime to provide relief. In the modern-day Syrian cataclysm, likewise, the oligarchs of the Assad regime responded to the hungry protesters who were out in the streets engaged in peaceful demonstrations by shooting and killing them. This obviously did not solve the problem. The recent rioting in Iraq and the economic disaster in Venezuela also come to mind.

The typical result of these traumatic political upheavals is a cure that may be just as bad as the disease for the aggrieved population – like the Reign of Terror and the so-called Thermidorian Reaction in France, the brutal tyranny and widespread suffering under Joseph Stalin in Russia and Mao Zedong in China, the genocide perpetrated by Pol Pot in Cambodia, and the many millions of casualties and refugees in Syria, along with the wholesale physical destruction of that country. In most of these revolutions, the ruling elite also pay the ultimate price. Call it the revenge of the masses

Just as the French Revolution was inspired in part by the model of the American Revolution, the British were affected in different ways by the revolution in France, and it precipitated a wave of political agitation and pamphleteering. Some observers were enthusiastic supporters, at first. Perhaps most famous was the prominent minister Richard Price (1789), whose essay "Discourse on the Love of Our Country" invoked the supremacy of freedom and inherent human rights, the right of the people to choose their leaders and oppose abuses of power, and the role of reason as a guide to political action. Price was seconded, among others, by the British/American revolutionary Thomas Paine (1791–2) in his essay on "The Rights of Man" and by Mary Wollstonecraft, also an early advocate for women's rights. However, as the revolution turned anarchic and bloody, some of the early supporters lost their enthusiasm.

A famous rejoinder essay, "Reflections on the Revolution in France," written by the statesman and political theorist Edmund Burke (2021/1790), went on to become a cornerstone of "Whig" (conservative) political thought down to the present day. Burke argued against permitting unrestrained freedom and free rein for personal self-interest, as opposed to our obligations to society. He stressed that it is better to adapt time-tested institutions and practices that embody the wisdom and experience of the past, rather than abandon them and start from scratch with abstract principles – and lethal conflict. Burke also emphasized the idea of a common good (see also Clark, 2001).

As always, the truth in this debate lies somewhere in the middle. Both points of view have merit. But Burke's core vision – often discounted by modern libertarians and liberals alike – is vitally important. It is rooted in a fundamental biological imperative that will play a significant part in the remaining sections of this Element. So, let me quote briefly from Burke's enduring conception of society as an organic whole, a social contract with a deep biological purpose:

> Society is indeed a contract ... [But] the state ought not to be considered as nothing better than a partnership in trade ... to be taken up for a little temporary interest, and to be dissolved by the fancy of the parties. As the ends of such a partnership cannot be obtained by many generations, it becomes a partnership not only between those who are living, but between those who are living, those who are dead, and those who are to be born. Each contract of each particular state is but a clause in the great primeval contract of eternal society. (Burke & Hamer, 1999: 368)

Burke (2021/1790) was not simply trying to justify the status quo. He also penned what has become one of the great axioms of political theory, an insight that has all too often been forgotten: "A state without the means of some change, is without the means of its conservation" (Burke, 2021/1790: 38).

What the many violent political traumas historically have taught us above all else is that every organized human society is, in effect, a social contract for the purpose of securing our basic biological survival and reproductive needs. And when any society fails to provide for the basic needs of its citizens, then the social contract is imperiled. Only coercion and repression (and/or inertia) may be able to hold it together. Or not.

"Our daily bread" could be called the "red line" for the elite in every society. There must be "bread for all . . . before cake for anybody," as William Beveridge put it in his famous World War Two (1942) blueprint for the postwar welfare state in Great Britain. A winner takes all, "survival of the fittest" (or the richest) social philosophy that denies the basic needs of the rest of us will lead to the ruin of all. Witness the Irish potato famine, where many millions died of hunger and disease while their English overlords did nothing to help – which led ultimately to the Irish Rebellion, Irish independence, and to deep and enduring cultural scars. It can be seen also in the Syrian conflict, in the Russian, Chinese, and Cuban revolutions, and in nearby Venezuela today. The right to life takes precedence over property rights. Ayn Rand – the twentieth-century Russian/ American novelist and elitist who became required reading for political conservatives, the captains of industry, and right-wing politicians – is a false god (see Corning, 2023b).

So too will ruination follow from a "let them eat cake" attitude in the relations between nations. Our greatest challenges going forward will involve global problems – meaning that they have been jointly created and/or span national borders (like climate warming, sea-level increases, and freshwater depletion) and so must the solutions. This was highlighted by the famed ecologist Garrett Hardin (1968) in his legendary paper "The Tragedy of the Commons." As Hardin put it, "Freedom in a Commons brings ruin to all." If we do not rein in the global anarchy that currently exists, then an every nation for itself approach to our problems may well bring ruin to all. Or worse yet, a global conflagration. The next 9/11 terrorist attack will not target something symbolic, like the World Trade Center. It will be aimed at vital institutions and infrastructure (like power grids) using cyberweapons and weapons of mass destruction. And this could be just the opening gun – a global Fort Sumpter, if you happen to be an American Civil War buff. The nightmare threat of a nuclear Armageddon is back on the table, and the rise of artificial intelligence in warfare is making this threat all the more serious.

The values associated with modern "shareholder" capitalism are also a part of the problem. Capitalism is at once an ideology, an economic system, a bundle of technologies, and an elaborate superstructure of institutions, laws, and practices that have evolved over hundreds of years. It has the cardinal virtues of rewarding innovation, initiative, and personal achievement. It has greatly influenced our economic development (see Beinhocker, 2006). But it is grounded in a set of values that, if unchecked, can be destructive to the survival of our species, and to many other species as well. This must change. Our economic system must serve our society, not the other way around (see Korten, 2015a, 2015b).

In the idealized capitalist model, an organized society is essentially a marketplace where goods and services are exchanged in arm's-length transactions among autonomous "purveyors" who are independently pursuing their own personal self-interests. This hypothetical model is in turn supported by the assumption that our motivations can be reduced to the efficient pursuit of our individual "tastes and preferences" – as the economists like to say. This is all for the best, or so it is claimed, because it will, on balance, produce the "greatest good for the greatest number," the Holy Grail of classical utilitarian political theory.

A corollary of this model is that there should be an unrestrained right to private property and the accumulation of wealth, because (in theory) this will aggregate the capital needed for further economic growth and ultimately benefit society as a whole. The foundational expression of this model, quoted in virtually every introductory economics textbook these days, is Adam Smith's (1964/1776) "invisible hand" metaphor in his famous book, *The Wealth of Nations*. As Smith (1964/1776: IV, 2, 9) explained: "By pursuing his own self-interest ... [a man] frequently promotes that of the society more effectively than when he really intends to promote it."

"Utopian capitalism," as it is sometimes derisively called, does not actually work according to this idealized model, and neither do societies – as many social critics have stressed over the years. Among other things, capitalism in practice is shaped by the pervasive and inescapable influence of wealth and power. It also systematically favors capital over labor, with results that are evident in the skewed economic statistics and widespread poverty that exists in many rich capitalist countries today. Senior economist John Gowdy candidly acknowledges that "Economic theory not only describes how resources are allocated, it provides a justification for wealth, poverty, and exploitation." (Gowdy, 1998: xvi–xvii). In fairness, Adam Smith himself also stressed the importance of justice and moral behavior (as economist Geoff Hodgson has reminded me in a personal communication).

To be sure, modern capitalism comes in many different sizes and shapes, from the millions of small mom-and-pop businesses with only one or a few workers to huge international conglomerates with hundreds of thousands of employees worldwide. But, for every Google that provides a cornucopia of perks for its employees, there are other global corporations that are single-mindedly devoted to an iron triangle of selfish values, namely: (1) maximizing growth, (2) maximizing efficiency, and (3) maximizing profitability for the owners/managers and shareholders. In these companies, the workers come last and, these days, they are often being replaced by technology, or their jobs are being "outsourced" to countries where workers can be paid much less.

In many cases, these large corporations also try to avoid responsibility for bearing the cost of what the economists call "externalities" – like damage to the environment, or physical harm to the health of the general public and local communities. Or paying taxes.

In most Western industrial societies – and increasingly in the global economy as a whole – the overall economic pie has been growing larger over the past 200 years, and political compromises for the common good have been less onerous and confiscatory than they are likely to be going forward. Now, we face increasing scarcities, a greater number of life-threatening (and costly) climate calamities, and a hard ceiling to further growth. The future is not what it used to be!

It has long been an article of faith in capitalist societies that the all-purpose solution to our problems is economic growth and progress. Only by increasing "The Wealth of Nations" (to borrow Adam Smith's title) will we eventually be able to solve the problems of poverty, disease, and hunger in a world that is "ill-housed, ill-clad, ill-nourished," as President Franklin Roosevelt put it in his second inaugural address. However, it has long been apparent to the scientific community that this approach is flawed. We will ultimately need to make a major course change.

An end to economic growth has been predicted ever since the famous "Limits to Growth" models were developed by a team of scientists at MIT in the 1970s (see Meadows et al., 2004). Although these early models were flawed and much criticized, their basic conclusion remains inescapable. To paraphrase an old saying: If something can't go on forever, it won't. Or, as the well-known economist Kenneth Boulding famously remarked: "Anyone who believes that exponential growth can go on forever in a finite world is either a madman or an economist." It is now obvious that we do indeed live in a finite world and that "forever" has a limited shelf life; its "best by" date has already arrived (see Felber, 2015; Monbiot, 2017; O'Neill et al., 2018).

There is another old saying that is also relevant here: When the pie gets smaller, the table manners change. This is the root of our collective dilemma going forward. If we hope to avoid a Malthusian dark age – a world society that has been cratered by severe deprivation, widespread suffering, lethal conflict on a global scale, and a devolution of the community of nations into a competitive free-for-all (or worse) – we will need to learn how to put a cap on growth, redistribute a smaller pie more widely, and use it much more efficiently. And, of course, we must urgently put an end to global warming.

This will require a major economic and political change of course, and it must go beyond the currently fashionable concept of "sustainable development." Ever since this eco-friendly term was popularized in the 1980s, there has been a lot of lip service and public relations posturing about the need to reconcile the traditional capitalist aspiration for economic development with respect for ecological constraints and limits. In practice, though, sustainability has all too often been sublimated or even ignored, while unrestrained economic growth (and increasing wealth) has remained the primary objective in most capitalist countries. As the environmental philosopher Arran Gare (2017) points out in a major critique, the traditional capitalist emphasis on growth has been largely unimpeded over the past thirty years, while the goal of achieving sustainability has failed "dismally." Gare (2017: 131), and other critics, propose that we abandon the concept altogether as an organizing principle: "The struggle for survival is being lost," he says. (Gare, and others, most notably the Chinese government, have embraced an alternative vision of an "ecological civilization.")

I have a somewhat different view of the matter. The definition of sustainable development was originally popularized by a 1987 report from a UN commission on the environment and development (United Nations 1987), the so-called Brundtland Report. It did not talk about economic growth. It talked about "development that meets the needs of the present without compromising the ability of future generations to meet their own needs." Indeed, the Brundtland Report stressed that the needs of the poor should be the "overriding priority." In other words, sustainable development should be focused on meeting basic needs, not on economic "growth" or increased "wealth." A more conventional, capitalist, growth-oriented interpretation of the term came later. We should return to the UN's original definition of sustainable development and make basic needs our primary imperative.

However, if we want to ensure that the basic needs of humankind (i.e., the common good) are provided for, we must do much more than shift our economic priorities. We must create a new global social contract and, ultimately, a political regime that is able to implement it – a global superorganism. This political change of course may seem like an "impossible dream," because the world now appears to be going in the opposite direction. In addition to the ever-growing extremes of wealth and poverty, there is currently an ominous trend toward a zero-sum global politics. The potential for mutually destructive conflict – both internally and between countries – is growing ever stronger (see Ellis, 2018). I will talk much more about this urgent problem in the remaining sections.

4 "Unite or Die"

As the delegates from the thirteen American colonies gathered in Philadelphia in 1776 to sign the Declaration of Independence – an act of treason against the English Crown – Benjamin Franklin warned them all, using a pun, according to legend, to make his point, "We must all hang together, or most assuredly we will all hang separately." (Franklin also inspired the revolutionary era slogan "Unite or Die," along with the famous political cartoon showing a snake cut into segments symbolizing the divisions among the separate colonies.) Franklin's sage advice about cooperation can be updated: we must all survive together, or most assuredly we will all go extinct separately.

The overarching question we face collectively is this: Will we go into our deeply challenging future together as "us", or will it be as "us vs. them"? If we act as a cooperative global community, with all of us having a stake in the outcome, then transformative positive changes are possible, and a brighter future beckons. It may even be possible to achieve a sustainable global super-organism. But if we define the challenge in competitive terms as a zero-sum game, then battle lines will be drawn, social and political conflict will be inevitable, and there may eventually be an all-consuming struggle. As the global crisis becomes greater and the stakes get higher, so will the mortal threat to us all. Indeed, our current global system of competitive nation-states makes this outcome much more likely.

A symptom of this menacing dynamic is China's ambitious "Belt and Road Initiative," which evokes its ancient trading prowess and its original Silk Road to Europe many centuries ago. At heart, this policy is part of an expansive nationalistic enterprise that is likely to become more threatening to other nations over time, despite China's assurances to the contrary. Indeed, the recent demonstrations and rioting in Hong Kong, and China's pushback and virtual coup, were a further sign of China's new assertiveness. Especially alarming are the concentration camps that have been established by the Chinese authorities to "reeducate" the twelve million Chinese Uighurs, mainly in Xinjiang Province.

If the world follows an "us vs. them" dynamic going forward, our trust in one another will inevitably be guarded and fragile, even among some of those we now consider to be "us." Any boundary line between us and them is labile; it can be moved at any time. (As we know, there are already deep fault lines in many countries, where minorities are treated as less equal than the rest of "us.") And in countries where the social contract has become frayed or has even broken down, we may feel free to exploit others whenever we can – and vice versa! Worse still, we may redefine as "them" anyone whose resources we covet and disregard the hunger, suffering, and deaths we cause among those who do not directly serve our interests, or who get in our way. Some of us already do this, of course, (e.g., Russia in Ukraine) but the problem is likely to get far worse.

However, the reality is that our vital interests are much more closely tied together than many of us realize. We are inescapably interdependent. For better or worse, we have a shared fate, and we can ignore this reality only at our peril. Let's take a closer look at this pivotal assertion.

The process of "globalization" – knitting the world together into an inter-dependent, superorganic whole – began in ancient times (about 50 BC) with trade relationships between Rome, Africa, and India, and with the original Silk Road overland from China to Europe. By the fifteenth century, Chinese fleets with huge sailing vessels had established many overseas trading routes. Then China retreated and turned inward under an imperial decree. The European voyages of discovery in the sixteenth century reenergized the process, and this soon led to the development of an overseas network of trade in various com-modities. However, it also incited a competitive scramble for colonies and empires between rival European nations, which contributed to the two cata-strophic world wars of the twentieth century.

Although the European imperial system was dismantled after World War Two, there remains to this day a dense network of overseas dependencies between various countries in relation to such important commodities as sugar, coffee, tea, spices, raw cotton, silk, rubber, minerals, metal ores, lumber, fossil fuels, and, most critically, food products. The UK, for example, imports some 40 percent of its food. China imports about 80 percent of the world's total soybean crop, mainly to feed its livestock, while the United States imports more than one-half of its fruits and one-third of its vegetables. All told, some thrity-seven countries with about 1.4 billion people are currently listed as being unable to grow all their own food.

This deep and enduring trade interdependency has now become far greater and more complex. Globalization today is a process with many dimensions, and many linkages. Manfred Steger (2013), in his definitive book-length study of this process, *Globalization*, characterizes it as a "great convergence" – a tapestry with many different strands. Here is just a brief look at some of these strands.

4.1 Economics

This all-important category has many facets. In 2018, international trade in goods and services represented about one-quarter of total global GDP of some US$86 trillion dollars, including US$1.5 trillion in food and $1.7 trillion in other agricultural products. (A trillion dollars is equivalent to one thousand billion.) International travel and tourism (including indirect expend-itures like food, recreation, clothing, and "visitor exports") represented another 10 percent of the world's total GDP (about US$8.8 trillion) and accounted for an estimated 315 million jobs, or almost 10 percent of all global employment in that year. Noncash overseas transactions alone (mostly credit and debit cards) amounted to about US$600 billion in 2018, while international business investments totaled US$1.8 trillion. (The cumulative foreign investment between countries over the past decade is estimated to be more than US$10 trillion.) The sum total of all foreign exchange monetary trading in 2019 surged to a staggering US$6.6 trillion per day, on average. Equally significant, developing countries have a combined international indebtedness of about US$6.8 trillion. (By 2021, total global GDP had increased to about US$96 trillion.)

Our global economic interdependence is also evident in the growing role (and power) of transnational corporations (often called TNCs). In 1970, there were only about 7,000 of these. By 2015, the number of TNCs had increased to over 100,000, with the largest 200 firms alone accounting for over half the world's total industrial output. The top ten TNC companies, including familiar names like Apple, Microsoft, and Johnson & Johnson, have market values that are larger than the GDP even of some mid-sized countries like Turkey, Austria, Chile, and Finland. Thus, the business strategies, resource purchases, manufacturing locations, component supply chains, marketing efforts, and labor practices of the TNCs have a huge impact on the global economy.

One measure of this impact can be seen in the role of container ships. After shipping containers were introduced in the 1950s, the time required for overseas transport plunged by about 85 percent and the cost per ton declined by 35 percent. Sixty years later, our global container ship infrastructure is valued at US$4 trillion. It includes about 450 ports and some 5,000 huge container ships which (currently) move more than 1.6 billion metric tons of cargo every year compared to 330 million tons in 1950, or about five times as much.

4.2 Politics

The nation-state remains a central actor in global politics, but it is increasingly hemmed in, constrained, and superseded by a great many external economic and political obligations and pressures that are beyond the control even of the largest superpowers. Despite the recent upsurge of nationalism in parts of the West – animated by a combination of extreme economic inequality and insecurity, a perceived refugee threat, and a reaction against liberal immigration policies – there is nevertheless an ever-thickening web of transnational organizations, agreements, rules, and norms that amount to a process of piecemeal growth in global self-governance and a global superorganism.

This process began, perhaps, with the amorphous domain of "international law" that dates back to the Treaty of Westphalia in 1648. International law is not, in fact, a body of codified laws but an evolving set of mostly consensual agreements, rules, norms, and practices that were related initially to the conduct of war but have gradually expanded to include a range of conflicts between nations, from territorial disputes and labor practices to financial and environmental issues. Nowadays, disputes between nations can be arbitrated through the International Court of Justice in the Hague (in the Netherlands), which was established in 1921, while criminal actions (from crimes against humanity to genocide) can be prosecuted in the International Criminal Court, which dates from the 1990s.

In a similar way, a global regime governing the world's oceans began in a small way in the nineteenth century with an international agreement regarding navigational "rules of the road." The pact was designed primarily to prevent ships from colliding with one another at sea. Then, in 1994, a comprehensive international treaty – the UN Convention on the Law of the Sea (UNCLOS) – codified territorial boundaries, defined fishing rules, and spelled out the rights of coastal nations to claim seabed mineral resources, among other things. The Convention is also surrounded by a network of private organizations concerned with wildlife conservation, fisheries, reducing pollution, saving coral reefs, and more.

An even more extensive domain of global self-governance can be seen in the World Trade Organization (WTO). The traditional practice of erecting trade restrictions between nations to protect local industries was a major contributor to the Great Depression in the 1930s and World War Two. This motivated the victors, led by Britain and the United States, to establish a postwar trading regime dedicated to enhancing trade and reducing trade barriers. One result was the General Agreement on Tariffs and Trade (GATT) in 1948, and ultimately the more comprehensive WTO in the 1990s. The WTO provides broad regulation of international trade, along with a framework for negotiations and arbitrating disputes. It has been controversial from the start. Indeed, the loopholes – with exemptions for environmental protection and "national security," which the United States has invoked under President Trump's "trade war" – could be a road to the landfill for the WTO if these escape hatches are not closed.

The most visible and far-reaching step toward increased global governance is, of course, the UN itself. Established immediately after World War Two with the primary objective – lodged in the Security Council and General Assembly – of mediating conflicts between nations and preventing another destructive world war, the UN is supplemented by a wide range of special purpose agencies that play a many-faceted role in world affairs, like the United Nations Development Programme (UNDP), the United Nations Environment Programme (UNEP), the Food and Agriculture Organization (FAO), the World Health Organization (WHO), the International Postal Union, the World Meteorological Organization, the International Telecommunications Union, the International Civil Aviation

Organization (ICAO), and, of course, UNCLOS. Despite widespread disappointment with the UN's performance in respect to peacekeeping, the quiet work done by its many "alphabet soup" agencies provides a positive model of international cooperation. (Hold this thought.)

Then there is the European Union with its twenty-seven members (after "Brexit" by the UK), as well as the NATO alliance with thirty member states (and two more pending), plus regional organizations like the African Union, the Arab League, the Association of Southeast Asian Nations (ASEAN) and the Union of South American Nations (USAN). These days, there is also a growing number of cooperative bilateral relationships between cities, states, and provinces in different countries, not to mention the increasingly intense cooperation between police agencies around the world in this age of terrorism, international drug trafficking, and waves of refugees and illegal immigrants.

And let's not forget the landmark – though imperfect – Paris Climate Accord in 2015, where 195 nations pledged to undertake various (voluntary) efforts to curb global warming, followed by the 2018 update in Poland. However, the UN Climate Summit in the fall of 2019 was a disappointment. The COP15 biodiversity conference of 190 countries in Canada and the COP27 conference in Egypt, both in 2022, were more productive but still fell short of imposing mandatory changes. More hopeful was the landmark 2023 agreement by 190 countries to protect the biodiversity in the world's unprotected oceans.

In addition to these formal transnational agreements and institutions, there are a myriad of so-called nongovernmental organizations (NGOs) – mostly voluntary, not-for-profit groups – that encompass an enormous variety of social "missions" and provide many kinds of goods and services across national borders. Some are supported by corporations or traditional philanthropic organizations, like the Ford, Rockefeller, and Gates foundations, but many others depend on volunteers and one-off fundraising campaigns. A recent estimate puts the total number of NGOs at an astonishing ten million, although a large majority of these probably work only within their home countries and localities. They do everything from providing food assistance, like Oxfam, to underwriting education, health care, infrastructure improvements, agricultural development assistance, political advocacy, and much more. There are legitimate criticisms of NGOs, to be sure. They are not always altruistic, or effective. Sometimes they act in a dictatorial way, or even create new problems. Nonetheless, their global influence is important and growing.

Consider, for example, the Grameen Bank, founded in 1976 by the Nobel Peace Prize winning entrepreneur from Bangladesh, Muhammad Yunus. Dubbed "banker to the poor," Yunus created a nonprofit bank that specializes in making "microloans" to people in poor communities who want to start a small business. The idea took off, and as of 2017 the bank had 2,600 branches with nine million borrowers, as well as spin-off projects in forty other countries, including the United States. The bank also has a phenomenal 99 percent loan repayment rate so far, according to Yunus (2017).

One of the most notable recent examples of an NGO contribution to the global community was the successful effort (thus far), led by Doctors Without Borders and some 4,000 volunteers (physicians and other medical personnel), to combat the Ebola virus in West Africa. Ebola is both highly contagious and kills up to 90 percent of those who are infected. Doctors Without Borders, together with other organizations and volunteers, prevented what could have become a deadly global pandemic. A recent resurgence has presented new challenges, but a newly developed vaccine holds great promise.

4.3 Transportation and Communications

Travel across national borders has reached mind-boggling numbers. Of the total of 36.8 million commercial airline flights worldwide in 2017, an estimated 33,000 each day (or 12 million all told) crossed national borders. Between 2004 and 2017 the total number of international airline passengers a year more than doubled, from 1.9 billion to an estimated 4.1 billion. And this does not include corporate and private air travel, or flights by government agencies, or the vast tonnage of air cargo (an estimated sixty-three million metric tons in 2019). Or the countless trips between countries by cars, buses, trains, and cruise ships. We have become a globe-spanning community.

It almost goes without saying that our communications technologies are having a similar transformative effect on our global society. The number of internet users at the end of 2017 was 4.15 billion, or more than half of the estimated total world population. In the same year, the number of active Facebook members reached 3.1 billion (although there were also more than one billion fake bots), and the number of mobile phone users worldwide in 2019 was about 4.6 billion. Perhaps the single best measure of how our twenty-first-century communications technologies have been knitting the world together is the enormous audience for the 2022 World Cup competition – some 3.5 billion viewers. Equally important, these new communications technologies are having a huge impact in the world's poorest countries, enabling them to leapfrog the developmental process in many ways. In Africa, where many of the poorest countries are found, there are now over 450 million mobile phone subscribers who are using their phones to conduct business, transfer money, obtain health care information and consultations, gain an education and, increasingly, influence local politics.

The revolution in global communications has a double edge, of course. On the one hand, it provides access to an ever-growing storehouse of information; it facilitates and shapes our business and personal lives in many different ways; and it can be used as an organizing tool for just about any social purpose or political cause. On the other hand, it can also be used to spread "fake news"; it can empower people and governments that have sinister purposes; and it can be used as a powerful new tool of social control and manipulation, including cyberwarfare – as North Korea did to Sony and South Korean banks, and as Russia did in the 2016 and 2020 US elections, among other examples.

What all of this adds up to is a powerful momentum toward greater inter-dependence and integration as a global society – a global superorganism. It also means that we live in a far more complex and interconnected world than many of us may realize. This global system creates huge networks of synergy – unique combined effects that are otherwise unattainable – but it also creates vast inter-dependencies. All of us have an array of some fourteen distinct categories of basic needs, absolute requisites for our biological survival and well-being, and it is clear that the satisfaction of these needs in complex societies like our own depends on the skills and efforts of millions of other people (much of it invisible to us), including the work of a growing number of people and organizations in other countries. (We will come back to these basic biological needs in Section 5.) This is the reason why our emerging global superorganism can legitimately be charac-terized as a "collective survival enterprise." Moreover, and this point is crucial, our superorganism also depends on a complex environmental support system with many ecological interdependencies – as does all life on Earth.

However, the rapidly growing science of complexity teaches us that this emerging global superorganism is also highly vulnerable. A complex system may be subject to a catastrophic failure if even a single important part (or resource) fails (see Capra & Luisi, 2014). I call it "synergy minus one." Take away a wheel from an automobile, or a single weak link in a chain, or the water supply from any human community (like Hurricane Maria in Puerto Rico in 2022 or the dark scenario depicted in Section 1). We are ever-more susceptible to what can be called the paradox of dependency. The paradox arises from the fact that, the more valuable something is to us, the greater the cost of losing it.

A major example of this vulnerability can be seen in the Great Recession of 2008–12, which was triggered by a financial meltdown and a freezing-up of capital markets on Wall Street. Among the many adverse consequences were: overall global GDP sank by 4.2 percent; industrial output in various countries fell by 12–31 percent; and an estimated fifty million jobs were lost worldwide. The US unemployment rate jumped from 4.2 percent to 10.1 percent (or 16.3 percent if you count "discouraged" workers who left the labor force or could only find part time work), while the jobless rate in some European countries reached 25 percent. There were also many millions of personal and family traumas associated with losing jobs, personal savings, and homes to mortgage foreclosures. The United States alone had some 4 million foreclosures per year, as well as 2.5 million shuttered businesses, and a spike in "food deprivation" (hunger) to a peak of almost 50 million people. Millions of truly innocent children suffered. It is not surprising that this historic economic crisis – driven by greed, deception, corruption, and even illegal acts that were never punished – triggered angry political upheavals in various countries.

Another example of our collective vulnerability is the total blackout of electrical power in Puerto Rico after Hurricane Maria in 2017, a breakdown that took many months to repair. A follow-up study at Harvard University estimated that the number of excess deaths due to the power loss was over 4,600 (out of a population of 3.3 million), many of them from a lack of medical care after the disaster (Kishore et al., 2018). (A belated, somewhat suspect "official" tally later put the number at just under 3,000.) There were also severe food and water shortages, tens of thousands of islanders were made homeless, many thousands of others fled to the mainland, and an already struggling economy was further undermined. The total dollar amount required for recovery and rebuilding of the island has been estimated to be at least US$95 billion, with little of it paid for by insurance. And Puerto Rico was damaged by another hurricane in 2022. So, there may never be a full recovery.

Finally, there is the COVID-19 pandemic. Although the full toll has not yet been added up, it will be the deepest economic recession in history, with disrupted manufacturing, shuttered restaurants and theaters, a devastated tourism and travel industry, shortages and/or price spikes in many products, and a crisis in the health and medical sectors. Not to mention the many millions who have suffered and died from the coronavirus. A virus!

Even the super wealthy among us need to take notice. Call it the reality of survival in a complex, interdependent, disaster-prone world. The fantasy of retreating to a billionaire bunker, or a secluded private island, or perhaps an (eventual) escape to Mars ignores the fact that even the upper 1 percent, globally, depend on our economic system and our vast infrastructure – from food and water, to waste disposal, medical services, electrical power, transportation systems, and, oh yes, police officers, firefighters, trash collectors, farmers, and so on, ad infinitum. Consider this: the average food item in the United States is the product of an enormously complex system with many millions of workers and complex technologies, most of which depend on fossil fuels. Any given food item is typically handled and processed several times and travels over 1,000 miles before it is consumed. Only a small fraction (about

12 percent) of what we pay for food in a grocery store or a restaurant goes to the farmer. We live in an enormously complex collective survival enterprise.

Indeed, the wealth of the top 1 percent is inextricably tied to the fate of the rest of us. Their financial holdings and income mainly include such things as stocks and bonds; revenue generated from commercial investments; principal and interest payments from debtors who hold many millions of home mortgages, car loans, and the like; rental and leasing income; and revenues from business sales. Capitalism depends on customers! And debtors who can pay their bills. And trained and willing workers. And cooperation, social trust, and obedience to our laws and norms – what is often referred to these days as "social capital."

We also know that real property values can crater in an economic depression, and the more property you own, the bigger the crater may be. The favored safe haven of the rich, such as gold in various forms (and now high-end art and "collectibles"), cannot be used as a substitute for food, water, or electric power. They can only be used to purchase these things from somebody else who has them and who is willing to exchange them for your gold or your art. In all of the many collapsed and vanished societies in the past, we know of no case where the wealthy elite managed to survive and prosper. They only got tombs with more grave goods, and more art.

We are all in this thing together – the collective survival enterprise. It is "fake news" (or a "terminological inexactitude" in Winston Churchill's famous euphemism) to believe otherwise. And if you pursue your self-interest without regard for others, you will ultimately run afoul of their vital self-interests, and even very likely your own interests. It is time for our wealthy "job creators" (and their political allies) to outgrow the naïve fantasies of the elitist guru to whom they all genuflect – the twentieth-century novelist and high priestess of the billionaire class, Ayn Rand.

It may come as a surprise to learn that the survival enterprise in humankind entails no less than fourteen distinct categories of "basic needs" (I will discuss these further in the next section). It is, in fact, our basic biological needs, and the overarching survival problem, that lie at the core of the venerable concept of the "common good" – the fundamental social value that encompasses the things that affect all of us.

The concept of a common good has very deep roots. It was a central theme in the writings of Plato and Aristotle, and it has long been featured as a moral principle in Christianity. For instance, in his 2015 Encyclical Letter *Laudato Si'*, a major doctrinal pronouncement of the Catholic Church, Pope Francis explicitly called for a reorientation of our global economic system away from capitalism and self-interest toward serving the common good. The Pope also used this term no less than six times in his landmark 2016 speech to the US Congress. Likewise, evolutionary biologists, notably including the prominent theorist Egbert Leigh (1983, 1991), use the concept of the common good in relation to the problem of survival for any complex organism in the natural world, especially any socially organized species. The common good was also stressed by America's Founding Fathers, including James Madison, who wrote about it in *The Federalist* papers under the heading of the "public good." The US Constitution also proclaims that its fundamental objectives are "the general welfare" and the interests of "we the people."

Modern writers on the subject, such as Robert Reich (2018) in his recent book *The Common Good*, argue that it must also include shared social norms and operating principles – like cooperation, social trust, respect for law, telling the truth, inclusiveness, and perhaps even devotion to equal opportunity and political democracy. And, of course, we should follow the Golden Rule – do unto others as you would have them do unto you. The Golden Rule is a basic norm in virtually every culture and religion.

I prefer to package these principles and values under the heading of a "social contract" – another venerable idea that goes back at least to the Enlightenment philosopher Jean-Jacques Rousseau (1984/1762), and perhaps to ancient Greece. We should all respect basic social values because we have a common stake in preserving and advancing our collective survival enterprise, our superorganism, and we have a mutual obligation to do so under the social justice principle of *reciprocity* – one of the three moral precepts that are foundational for any society. (We will talk about the other two, *equality* and *equity*, in Section 5.) Our "social contract" is rooted in our shared biological purpose, our evolutionary heritage, and our interdependence. If we betray or reject this social contract, we are violating a set of ethical norms that may trace back 5–7 million years in a direct line of descent from our remote ancestors.

As I describe in detail in my book *Synergistic Selection: How Cooperation Has Shaped Evolution and the Rise of Humankind* (Corning, 2018) there have been three keys to our ancestors' extraordinary evolutionary success over time: close social cooperation, adaptive innovation, and synergy. As noted earlier, our remote ancestors, the australopithecines, were small (about three feet tall) and slow-moving. They could not have survived except by foraging together in cooperative groups and defending themselves collectively with the tools they invented for procuring food and for self-defense. The result was a game-changing synergy – cooperative outcomes that could not otherwise have been achieved.

The rest of the multi-million-year story of our evolution as a species followed this same basic formula. Cooperation and innovation were the underlying themes, and the synergies that were produced (the economic benefits) were the reason why our ancestors cooperated, and why they survived. Thus, the emergence of the much larger and bigger-brained *Homo erectus* some two million years ago was the result of a synergistic joint venture, namely, the hunting of big game animals in closely cooperating groups with the aid of an array of potent new tools – finely balanced throwing spears, hand axes, cutting tools, carriers, and (eventually) fire and cooking. Not to mention (quite likely) sequestered home bases, midwifery, and the first babysitting cooperatives. It was a collective survival enterprise, a superorganism, and it was sustained by multiple synergies.

The final emergence of modern humankind, perhaps as early as 300,000 years ago, represented a further elaboration of this collective survival strategy. Novel economic synergies enabled the evolution of much larger groups. Each "tribe" was, in effect, a coalition of many families that was sustained by a sophisticated array of new technologies – shelters, clothing, food process-ing, food preservation and storage techniques, and much else. Especially important were the more efficient new hunting and gathering tools, like spear throwers (which greatly increased their range and accuracy), bows and arrows, nets, traps, and a variety of fishing techniques. Indeed, culture itself (including spoken language) became a powerful engine of cumulative evolu-tionary change. Our collective survival enterprise – our superorganism – became an autocatalytic engine of growth and innovation (and environmental disruption) as synergy begat more synergy. Some anthropologists have invoked the idea of culture as a "collective brain."

Now, there is a human population of eight billion people, many of them living in dense supertribes supported by a mind-boggling array of complex technolo-gies and doomsday weapons. Meanwhile, the collective survival enterprise, as we have seen, has increasingly become a global undertaking. We are ever-more interdependent when it comes to meeting our basic survival and reproductive needs. And a key part of this survival strategy is an enormously complex – and synergistic – combination of labor which transcends our many cultural and political boundaries. It constitutes an emergent global superorganism.

Recent events suggest that this globalization process has been halted and perhaps even reversed – with nationalism on the rise, the emergence of new serious trade conflicts, and a trend toward right-wing authoritarian governments in Turkey, Hungary, Poland, the Philippines, Thailand, Russia, Brazil, China, Israel, the United States, and others. It is one of the axioms of political science that a collective threat to any group, organization, or nation will as a rule produce a surge of "patriotic" support for the group and its leaders, and a willingness to accept more centralized, hierarchical control. Authoritarian, "populist" leaders and demagogues thrive in societies that are under severe economic distress, or where there is an external threat. Political scientist Ronald Inglehart (2018) has amassed evidence spanning several decades and more than 100 countries that strongly confirms this political tendency. Inglehart calls it the "authoritarian reflex." Globalization authority Manfred Steger (2013) asks: "Will we tackle our global problems in a cooperative manner or are we on the brink of a new era of conflict that might halt the powerful momentum of globalization?"

Or much worse. As we have seen, our environmental crisis poses a huge threat to our collective future. It involves a set of menacing environmental challenges that could destroy our highly vulnerable global economy. We still have a choice, however. We can respond to this threat either with a competitive, survival of the fittest, "us vs. them" strategy, which could perhaps lead to the destruction of our global civilization, or we can adopt a common-good strategy that, as we shall see, utilizes the same game plan that has been the key to our evolutionary success as a species – cooperation, adaptive innovation, and synergy. It is also important to keep in mind that we share 99 percent (plus) of our genes in common and that the "us vs. them" syndrome is at heart a psychological, economic, and political phenomenon. It is very real but also notoriously labile. If our interests converge, "us vs. them" can quickly become only "us" – and vice versa! We define where the boundaries are.

The prominent twentieth century political economist Karl Polanyi (2001/ 1944) long ago warned us, in his classic study, *The Great Transition*, that extremes of wealth and poverty combined with widespread economic insecurity are a powder keg for violent conflicts, both within and between nations. If the current trends continue, the coming crisis will very likely unravel and shred our global superorganism. We have a life-and-death choice to make, both for ourselves and for our posterity.

5 Building a Superorganism

"What Is to Be Done?" This provocative question is the title of a famous pamphlet published in 1902 by the Russian revolutionary, Vladimir Lenin, while he was living in exile in Germany. (His title was taken from an earlier Russian novel.) The "burning question," to cite Lenin's term, was how to achieve a communist society in Russia. By then it was clear that it would not arise "spontaneously" via class conflict as the great theorist Karl Marx had supposed. Lenin saw the need to create an organized political party to serve as a revolutionary "vanguard." This idea proved to be a turning point. Lenin's pragmatic political strategy would be adopted by Communists everywhere in the twentieth century, and it played a decisive part in the Russian, Chinese, and Cuban revolutions.

The old saying that "the operation was a success, but the patient died" may be applicable here. Lenin's plan for achieving political power was brilliantly successful, but the Communist models of human nature and of a complex human society were deeply flawed. Radical economic and social equality and an economy organized around small voluntary "communes" never had a chance in a large industrial society. Once in power, the Communists moved quickly to do exactly the opposite. They imposed rigid centralized planning on a tightly organized, hierarchical economic system. Dubbed a "command economy" by Western economists, it worked for a while, but the patient eventually died.

Now it is time to pose Lenin's historic question once again. If pursuing the current economic and political status quo may well amount to an unwitting suicide pact, or the road to World War Three, what is the alternative? If the utopian, "free market" capitalist ideal is not the answer, and Ayn Rand's model is a con job on behalf of the favored few, we need to go back to the drafting table. And this time, because the stakes are so high, we need to get it right.

Let's begin with some biological fundamentals about the role of cooperation and synergy in evolution, as well as the rise of complexity in the natural world over time and the so-called major transitions in evolution, especially the emergence of superorganisms (again, see the detailed discussion in Corning, 2018). The traditional view of evolution, dating back to Darwin himself, is that there is a ruthlessly competitive "struggle for existence" (to repeat Darwin's catch phrase) – or "nature, red in tooth and claw" as in the oft-quoted poem by Alfred, Lord Tennyson. Call it the high testosterone model of evolution.

In the twentieth century, a modernized version of this paradigm, widely known as neo-Darwinism, shifted the theoretical focus to the competitive machinations of "selfish genes," according to the biologist/popularizer Richard Dawkins. In his best-selling book, *The Selfish Gene*, Dawkins (1989/ 1976: ix) famously claimed that "We are survival machines – robot vehicles blindly programmed to preserve the selfish molecules known as genes." He concluded: "I think 'nature red in tooth and claw' sums up our modern understanding of natural selection admirably" Dawkins (1989/1976: 2).

The problem with this all-out competitive model is that it represents a one-sided and simplistic caricature of an enormously complex, multileveled process which includes a great many different kinds of causal influences, from ecological factors to variations in physiology during development, behavioral innovations that can be game changers, and, especially important, the role of cooperative relationships and behaviors of various kinds (Corning, 1983, 2003, 2005, 2018, 2023; see also Margulis & Fester, 1991). It turns out that cooperation and competition have played co-starring roles in the evolutionary process. Indeed, one prominent biologist, Richard Michod (1999: xi), claims that "cooperation is now seen as the primary creative force behind ever greater levels of complexity and organization in all of biology." Another leading theorist (Martin Nowak) characterizes cooperation as "the master architect of evolution" (see Corning, 2018). (Indeed, even Darwin [1874/1871] himself understood the role of cooperation in evolution, especially in his later book,

The Descent of Man, as economist Geoff Hodgson reminded me in a personal communication.)

Yes, but, it is not cooperation per se that has been the creative "force," or the architect. Rather, it is the functional synergies – the unique combined effects produced by cooperation. Synergies of various kinds have been the underlying cause of cooperation and complexity in evolution, not the other way around. Cooperation may have been the vehicle, but synergy was the driver.

So, what is synergy? This term is only vaguely familiar to many of us. It is often associated with corporate mergers, or drug interactions, or some other commonplace example. In fact, synergy involves much more than that. It is actually a ubiquitous phenomenon. It is literally everywhere around us, and it represents one of the great governing principles in the natural world. It ranks right up there with such heavyweight concepts as gravity, energy, and information in explaining how the world works, although it often travels under various aliases – emergence, threshold effects, mutualism, density dependence, critical mass, cooperativity, even perfect storms. Indeed, over the course of time, synergies of various kinds have been a prodigious well-spring of creativity and innovation in the natural world. Again, I call it "nature's magic."

Synergy is often defined using a paraphrase of the ancient Greek polymath Aristotle – a whole that is greater than the sum of its parts (or 2+2=5). But this is actually a rather narrow and even misleading definition. Sometimes wholes are not greater than the sum of their parts, just different. A classic example, mentioned earlier, is water – a versatile liquid that is the combined product of two elemental gases. Water is not "greater than" hydrogen and oxygen. It is qualitatively different. For this reason, I prefer to define synergy more broadly. It refers to cooperatively produced effects of any kind that are not otherwise attainable.

There are, in fact, many different kinds of synergy. One of the most important is what we commonly refer to as a division of labor (again, I like to call it a "combination of labor"). A textbook example – literally – was provided by Adam Smith (1964/1776) in *The Wealth of Nations*. Smith reported that he had personally observed a pin factory where ten workers performing ten different tasks were able to manufacture about 48,000 pins per day. But if each of the laborers were to work alone, attempting to perform all the tasks required to make pins rather than working cooperatively, Smith doubted if, on any given day, they could produce even a single pin per man. How do we know the pin factory was synergistic? Just imagine what might happen if a key pinmaking machine broke down, or if its highly trained operator called in sick. The synergy would literally grind to a halt. "Synergy minus one."

A very different kind of synergy is involved in teamwork – say a tug-of-war – where everyone is pulling together in the same direction to produce a joint outcome. There are innumerable examples of teamwork in the natural world, from fish schools to bird flocks, collective mobbing behaviors, and the like.

There is also what are called threshold effects. One illustration can be seen in Pamela Allen's (1983) delightful children's story – *Who Sank the Boat?* – about what happened when all the animals decided to take a boat ride together. It was not the mouse, the last and the smallest of the animals to enter the boat, that was to blame for the disaster. But then you cannot blame the elephant either. It was a combined, synergistic effect.

Still another kind of synergy is associated with the way animals engage in joint environmental conditioning. For instance, the emperor penguins that live in the Antarctic are renowned for huddling together during the harsh winter months in dense colonies that can number in the tens of thousands. This enables them to share body heat and reduce their individual energy expenditures by 20–50 percent, depending on where they are in the huddle and the wind conditions (Le Maho, 1977). (Synergistic heat-sharing by humans is also commonplace. As noted earlier, it is even mentioned by Ecclesiastes in the Old Testament.)

Life has been a synergistic phenomenon from the get-go. Beginning with the very origins of life, perhaps 3.9 billion years ago, synergies of various kinds have played a key role in shaping the overall trajectory of life on Earth, including the rise of humankind, and it was the functional advantages produced by synergistic "cooperators" that drove this process. In effect, the parts (and their genes) became interdependent units of evolutionary change. The famed twentieth-century behaviorist psychologist, B. F. Skinner (1981) called it "selection by consequences."

An important example can be seen in how complex eukaryotic cells evolved from more primitive bacteria. In the natural world, there can be many advantages to being larger and having greater complexity, and eukaryotic cells, with their elaborate internal architecture, are some 10–15,000 times bigger on average than the typical bacterium. However, this huge size difference requires many orders of magnitude more energy, and the key to solving this critical need was a cooperative (synergistic) union between an ancestor of the eukaryotes and an ancestor of the specialized, energy-producing mitochondria that are found inside all mammalian cells, including our own. Not only was this potent new symbiotic relationship mutually beneficial for each of the partners, but it created a pathway for expanding and multiplying the benefits many times over. Some specialized cells in complex organisms like humans may contain hundreds, or even thousands, of energy-producing mitochondria. Liver cells, for instance, have about 2,500 mitochondria and muscle cells may have several times that number. It is what I like to call a "synergy of scale."

Biologists these days refer to the emergence of the eukaryotes as a "major transition" in evolution, after the term coined by two leading theorists, John Maynard Smith and Eörs Szathmáry (1995, 1999), in their two books on this subject back in the 1990s. A major transition occurs when a whole new level of biological organization arises that can act as a unified (synergistic) whole. There have been at least five major transitions in evolution so far (maybe six, it is debatable), and every one of them has been driven by a new combination of labor that produced powerful new synergies.

One of these major transitions involved the emergence of "superorganisms" – socially organized species. Although the term was first popularized by the English theorist Herbert Spencer in the nineteenth century, it was the ancient Greek philosopher Plato who first likened a complex society to an organism. The whole, including its division (combination) of labor, produces synergies that collectively benefit both the whole and its individual parts.

An often-cited example of a superorganism is the so-called leaf-cutter ant. Many millions of years ago, a tribe of New World ants developed a sophisticated form of agriculture which they pursue in huge underground cities (some of them bigger than a large house) with extensive tunnel systems and hundreds of large chambers where the ants carefully nurture symbiotic fungus "gardens" to produce food for themselves. A mature leaf-cutter colony, with a population of several million ants, has an impressive organization, including several anatomically specialized "castes" that work in flexible teams to perform an amazing variety of tasks: cutting, transporting, and pro-cessing leaves and grasses from hundreds of yards away; constructing elaborate "highways" above ground to facilitate foraging and transport; feeding the fungus gardens; feeding the queen (who devotes herself exclusively to produ-cing eggs at the rate of about twenty per minute, or ten million a year); feeding and nurturing the brood; digging out and removing soil to expand the colony and create additional garden chambers; cleaning out the garden and removing various wastes; fighting off various parasites and pathogens; and, of course, defending the colony against various predators and competitors. All of this activity is orchestrated and coordinated by a full repertoire of communications processes – chemical, visual, auditory, and tactile – usually in combination. Especially important is a bottom-up, collective decision-making process called "quorum sensing" (see Corning, 2018).

All of the individual ants in the colony have a shared fate. They contribute to the functioning of the whole in various ways and benefit hugely from the synergies that result. In their authoritative book on insect societies, aptly titled

The Superorganism, the biologists Bert Hölldobler and Edward O. Wilson (2009: 62) marvel at how the leaf-cutter colonies always seem to be able to do the right thing for their own survival: "Guided by instinct, the superorganism responds adaptively to the environment." A leaf-cutter ant colony is the quintessential collective survival enterprise. Indeed, some theorists view it as the ultimate superorganism. Wherever they are found, they are an important species.

An obvious question is how does a superorganism arise in the first place? The key factors are: (1) a shared set of interests related to survival and reproduction; (2) interdependence with respect to these shared interests; (3) cooperative synergies that are mutually beneficial; and (4) "governance" – effective coordination, regulation, and policing of cheaters and "free-riders" (to borrow a term from the economists). Indeed, effective governance is an indispensable requirement. (Hold that thought.)

Complex human societies obviously resemble leaf-cutter colonies in some important ways. We share the same basic biological challenge of survival and reproduction. A complex human society is, first and foremost, a multigenerational collective survival enterprise. (Remember Edmund Burke's famous description.) We also benefit in a multitude of ways from having a division/combination of labor (Henrich, 2016). But there are also some major differences compared to, say, leaf-cutter ants.

Perhaps most important is the fact that we do not have a reproductive specialization (although some royal "harems" in ancient societies may have given us an approximation). Our species has evolved for the most part as superorganisms that are, in effect, coalitions of individual families that reproduce independently but benefit from various forms of social and economic cooperation and synergy. A human superorganism can truly be characterized as a "biosocial contract." This unique social arrangement, along with our remarkable communication and cultural skills, is why some theorists claim that humankind represents a sixth major transition in evolution.

Humans are also unique in that, as our societies have grown larger and vastly more complex in recent times, we have evolved into what amount to multileveled superorganisms. For almost all of the past 5–7 million years, our ancestors lived in small, close-knit, highly cooperative bands of perhaps 25–30 individuals. With the emergence of the first modern *Homo sapiens*, some 250–300,000 years ago, the size of our superorganisms gradually increased to about 75–100 members, roughly the same size as the hunter-gatherer societies that still exist today. Then a radical change occurred. With the development of agriculture and the rise of large, complex, technological societies over the past 10,000 years, our superorganisms have also been transformed. They often contain a complex layer cake of social, economic, and governmental subunits.

From a biological perspective, a human superorganism is a bundle of paradoxes. We share three of the four key attributes of all other superorganisms – a deeply shared interest in biological survival and reproduction, intense cooperation and interdependence with respect to meeting our basic needs, and a superabundance of beneficial synergies. At the same time, we can also be highly individualistic and competitive; we often engage in civil wars between rival families, groups, and organizations; and we frequently display extremes of self-serving greed and a disregard for our fellow citizens, even to the point of causing harm to the superorganism itself. On the other hand, we are also capable of remarkable acts of altruism and self-sacrifice for the common good.

Perhaps the most important distinction is that human superorganisms frequently have a serious governance problem – a basic structural deficiency that leaf-cutter ants, for example, do not have. This defect arises from the fact that our superorganisms are not composed of closely related biological siblings hatched from the same queen; they are alliances of separate individuals and families bound together in an economic and social contract.

As Aristotle (1946/ca. 350 BC, 1961/ca. 350 BC) put it, humans are a uniquely political animal – *zoon politikon*. We are not "guided by instinct." We do not mindlessly track chemical pheromone trails. We are certainly not "robot vehicles" as Richard Dawkins would have it (although some robot vehicles now seem to be joining us). For better *and* worse, we are guided by politics. The traditional view among students of animal behavior has been that the social decision-making systems that exist in other primate species – like baboons or chimpanzees – involve an authoritarian dominance hierarchy maintained by physical threats and coercion. But we now know it is not so simple as that. Some primate societies are more flexible, and "democratic," and may even be ruled by coalitions. However, our own hominin ancestors developed a political system that is unique. In a series of landmark studies many years ago, the anthropologist Christopher Boehm (1999) documented the fact that modern hunter-gatherer societies are not only highly egalitarian but also exhibit what he called a "reverse dominance hierarchy" – social coalitions that actively contain and suppress aggressive individuals and rogue leaders.

Thus, it appears that a more democratic and consensual governance pattern is deep-rooted in our species. The evolution of egalitarian political systems among our remote ancestors – based on a leader's skills, experience, and "prestige" rather than physical dominance – might even trace back to the australopithecines of the early Pliocene era, some five million years ago. Close social coordination would have been essential for cooperative foraging and survival in a dangerous savanna environment, and this would have favored collective governance. There is also much evidence that cohesive groups can make better decisions than individuals by themselves. The synergies achieved by effective social cooperation may even have given these ancestral hominin groups a major advantage – a cultural dynamic that has been termed "synergistic selection" (Maynard Smith, 1982)

With the invention of agriculture, animal husbandry, and the rise of large, complex societies, our ancestral governance systems also changed radically. It is ironic that the very factors that contributed to our economic progress as a species also created opportunities for economic exploitation, social inequality, and political domination. In effect, the reverse dominance hierarchies that had long ensured against great differences in power (and wealth) in traditional foraging and hunter-gatherer societies began to break down. Voluntary consent gave way to top-down coercive force, and the traditional pattern of informal social controls and conflict resolution was replaced over time by formal law codes, religious edicts, aggressive policing, and harsh punishments.

To be sure, there are examples of evolving complex human societies where ambition, personal achievement, and social prestige did not result in an authoritarian political hierarchy and extreme inequality – like the ancient Harappan civilization of the Indus River valley. Far more common, though, were transitions that allowed various leaders to control resources and to become self-aggrandizing and self-perpetuating. This was evidently the case even in some of the earliest agricultural villages that began to appear roughly 10,000 years ago in Mesopotamia.

One illustration of how this transition occurred can be seen in the story of the Native American Chumash people of Southern California (Arnold, 2001). Although the Chumash had lived in this region for 5,000 years as nomadic foragers, their lifestyle changed radically around 900 AD, after they invented large, ocean-going plank canoes (complete with skillful caulking) that required a dozen crewmen and could carry a ton of cargo. This impressive new technology was a game changer. It enabled the Chumash to venture out to sea as far as sixty-five miles to catch the abundant quantities of large, deep-sea fish, like giant tuna and swordfish. This food surplus, in turn, allowed the Chumash to establish larger, settled villages that could support various crafts industries and trade relationships with their neighbors. However, it also enabled the canoe owners/captains to control the food supply and amass personal fortunes, along with multiple wives. As the other villagers became more dependent on the canoe captains, they were also reduced to subservience, and this quickly evolved into in a new pattern of authoritarian leadership.

Today, extremes of wealth and poverty, coupled with hierarchical systems of political control, are the rule in modern societies. Although we have, over the past two millennia, invented a variety of political workarounds to contain this tendency– the rule of law, representative legislatures, free election systems, an independent judiciary, formal constitutions that set limits on government power, a free press, etc. – these safeguards have all too easily been coopted or corrupted and have often been replaced by an assortment of authoritarian, elitist, or simply corrupt and dysfunctional governments, as we have recently witnessed. The superorganisms that we call modern nation-states range from some that have been highly successful in securing the common good, to many others that, for various reasons, have been completely subverted.

Now, in the twenty-first century, there is an urgent need to reform our many sick superorganisms. One estimate puts the total number of dysfunctional states as high as sixty. More important, and far more consequential for our future as a species, we must figure out how to govern our emerging global superorganism. "Government is the problem," but for a very different reason from that which President Ronald Reagan had in mind when he coined this slogan in the 1980s. We need to assert the primacy of the common good, arrest the current trend toward authoritarian, corrupt, and exploitative regimes, and reform a capitalist system that sometimes seems to be providing "the greatest good for the fewest number" (to flip the famous utilitarian mantra) (see Porritt, 2005; Monbiot, 2017; Raworth, 2018, Reich, 2018).

What is to be done? The ultimate answer must be a new global social contract in which everyone has a stake, everyone benefits proportionately, and everyone contributes proportionately. I call it a "biosocial contract," because it must be grounded in the fundamental biological purpose of our superorganisms and must give our basic biological survival needs the highest priority. These basic needs represent a nonnegotiable foundation for the common good. They are absolute requisites for the survival and reproduction of every individual and of every society over time. Furthermore, we spend most of our daily lives involved in activities that are either directly or indirectly related to satisfying these needs, including (not least) earning a living and contributing in various ways to help sustain the collective survival enterprise and our superorganism.

As I mentioned earlier, there are at least fourteen distinct domains, or categories, of basic human needs. (My list was developed and vetted over many years at the Institute for the Study of Complex Systems and is convergent with the UN's Human Development Index and the new Social Progress Index; see Corning, 2011.) Our basic biological needs include a number of obvious categories, such as adequate nutrition, fresh water, waste elimination, physical safety, physical health, and mental health, as well as some items that we may take for granted, such as maintaining our body temperature (or "thermoregulation," which includes various technologies, from clothing to blankets, firewood, heating oil, and air conditioning). Our basic needs even include adequate sleep (about one-third of our lives), mobility, and healthy respiration, which cannot always be assured these days. Less obvious, perhaps, but most important are the requirements for reproducing and nurturing the next generation. In other words, our basic biological needs cut a very broad swath through our economy and our society. (These fourteen needs are discussed in detail in Corning, 2011.)

To repeat, the basic challenge for every human society is to provide for the basic survival and reproductive needs of its members. This is our prime directive, our raison d'être. A reformulated social contract focused on the common good must therefore start with a universal "basic needs guarantee."

This is a foundational social principle, and it is grounded in four key propositions: (1) our basic needs are increasingly well understood and documented; (2) although our individual needs vary somewhat, in general they are shared by all of us; (3) we are dependent upon many others, and increasingly our global economy as a whole, for the satisfaction of these needs; and (4) severe harm (or death) may result if any of these needs is not satisfied. Equally important, satisfying our basic needs is a prerequisite for achieving the voluntary "consent" of the governed and a "legitimate," sustainable superorganism. It is the essential antidote to anarchy and authoritarianism alike – not to mention the growing problems of global hunger and climate refugees.

The idea of providing everyone with a basic needs guarantee may seem radically new – a utopian moral aspiration, or perhaps warmed-over Marxism. However, it is important to stress that this would not be an open-ended commitment. And it is emphatically not about an equal share of wealth. It refers specifically to the fourteen domains of basic needs cited above. Our basic needs are not a vague theoretical abstraction, nor a matter of personal preference. They constitute a concrete but limited agenda, with measurable indicators for evaluating outcomes.

A basic needs guarantee also has strong public support. For instance, a famous series of social experiments first conducted by political scientists Norman Frohlich and Joe Oppenheimer (1992) and subsequently replicated (and confirmed) many more times in various countries, found that 78 percent of participants overall favored providing a basic economic "floor" for everyone. Likewise, a recent public survey by researchers at Harvard University showed that 47 percent of young people in the United States between the ages of eighteen and twenty-nine agreed with the proposition that our basic needs should be treated as a right that government should provide to those who are unable to afford them (Halpin et al., 2021). And a 2019 Pew Research Center poll found that 89 percent of Democrats and 67 percent of Republicans supported either spending the same amount or increasing public spending for needy people. There is also growing interest these days in the convergent idea of providing everyone with a "universal minimum income." This is an old idea that has enlisted many prominent advocates over the years, although it would not be sufficient by itself, as we shall see.

The argument for a basic needs guarantee also accords with the "right to life" principle, first proposed by the philosopher John Locke (1970/1690) in his *Two Treatises of Government* and subsequently enshrined in the American Declaration of Independence in 1776. The right to life has since been invoked in many other contexts as well, starting with the UN Universal Declaration of Human Rights in 1948. But if the right to life is widely recognized as a self-evident moral principle (although it is often betrayed in practice), it certainly does not end at birth; it extends throughout our lives. Moreover, it is a prerequisite for other rights, including liberty and "the pursuit of happiness" (or property rights, for that matter). The right to life necessarily also implies a right to the means for life – the wherewithal. Otherwise, this right is meaning-less. And because almost all of us are dependent upon the collective survival enterprise (the superorganism) to obtain the goods and services required for satisfying our basic needs, the right to life imposes upon society and its members a lifelong mutual obligation to provide for one another's needs. This implicit contractual obligation, though often betrayed, has been the moral foundation for hominin societies ever since the Pliocene.

One obvious objection to creating a basic needs guarantee is that it may seem like a giveaway. It would invite free riding. Where is the fairness in that? The answer, as noted earlier, is that social justice has at least three distinct aspects. Our basic needs take priority, but it is important to recognize that there are differences in *merit* among us, and to reward (or punish) them accordingly. The principle of "just deserts" also plays a major role in our social relationships. Equally important, there must be reciprocity – an unequivocal commitment on the part of all of us (with some obvious exceptions like young children, the aged, and the infirm) to help support the collective survival enterprise. We must all contribute a fair share toward balancing the scale of benefits and costs. We must reciprocate for the benefits that we receive from society through such things as our labor, the taxes we pay, public service – and "playing by the rules," of course.

Accordingly, the biosocial contract contains three social justice principles that must be bundled together and balanced. A shorthand version of these, again, is *equality, equity,* and *reciprocity* (they are discussed at length in Corning, 2011). Specifically: (1) goods and services must be distributed to each according to his or her basic needs (in this respect, there must be *equality*); (2) surpluses beyond the provisioning of our basic needs must be distributed according to "merit" (there must also be *equity*); (3) in return, each of us is obligated to contribute to the collective survival enterprise proportionately in accordance with his or her ability (there must be *reciprocity*). As detailed in Corning (2011), these three fairness precepts are backed by a growing body of social science research.

Going forward, a basic needs guarantee must become the moral foundation for every human society – and for our emerging global superorganism. It provides specific content for the Golden Rule and a shopping list for the Good Samaritan. It reflects the fundamental purpose of the collective survival enterprise, and it represents perhaps our greatest ethical and political challenge. A basic needs guarantee is also an absolute prerequisite for achieving the level of social trust, harmony, and legitimacy that will be required to heal our deep social and political divisions (and conflicts) and respond effectively to our growing environmental crisis. Indeed, it is also the key to solving the spreading problem of civil turmoil and the recent surge in climate refugees. It is a goal that will obviously take many years to achieve, but we must begin now. To borrow a punch line from *The New York Times* columnist Tom Friedman, "later will be too late."

But this is not enough. The second of the three social justice precepts I cited, rewards for merit (or equity), is also vitally important to achieving a fair society. The giving of rewards for personal achievements is one of the cardinal virtues of capitalism – in theory. But modern capitalism has become increasingly skewed – even a threat in some cases to the superorganism and our prime directive. There is now an urgent need to reform our global economic system and tether it more tightly to the common good and our basic needs, starting with climate change.

The achievements of capitalism at its best are undeniable. An open, innovative, competitive economic system can play a vital role in serving our basic needs, and it excels at rewarding personal and economic achievements. However, capitalism can also become a rigged game that is far removed from the idealized model of mutually beneficial, win–win exchanges and optimal outcomes for all concerned, much less the principle of equity, or merit. Among other things, the vast differences among us in wealth, power, and information can exert a highly corrosive influence in the marketplace, and in our political systems. Many different adjectives have been used to describe these perversions: crony capitalism, klepto-capitalism, mafia capitalism, ersatz capitalism, casino capitalism, permissive capitalism, subsidized capitalism, and others. They flout the basic principles of social justice that I have outlined.

However, there is an alternative model that also preserves the spirit of capitalism at its best. Although it is not universally appreciated, capitalism comes in two very different flavors, commonly known as "shareholder capitalism" and "stakeholder capitalism." These terms refer to two very different ideals about which kind of economic values and practices a business firm should pursue, and both models have played a significant role in shaping the behavior of our large, publicly traded firms over time, as well as the outcomes for our society (see especially Kelly et al., 1997; Ackerman & Alstott, 1999; Beinhocker, 2006; Corning, 2018).

With stakeholder capitalism, the basic idea is that everyone who has an interest, or stake, in a business firm – managers, workers, subcontractors, suppliers, customers, shareholders, the government, and, of course, society as a whole – should have an influence (formal or informal) on its governance and behavior and receive a fair share of the benefits. This was the dominant model in the United States (though with a different name) during the years immediately after World War Two.

The alternative model, now called shareholder capitalism, formally dates from a landmark article in 1962 by the Nobel Prize winning University of Chicago economist Milton Friedman (1962: 133): "There is one and only one social responsibility of business," he declared, "to increase its profits." Anything else is "unadulterated socialism." In other words, capitalism must have a single-minded focus on profits and the interests of shareholders over any other stake-holders. It even rejects the very idea of a public interest or common good.

In the two decades that followed the Milton Friedman article, the ecosystem for American corporations was radically altered by a tidal wave of foreign competition, deregulation, and the rise of predatory corporate raiders. Shareholder capitalism gave large corporations a rationale for outsourcing production, undercutting labor unions, squeezing worker wages, reducing fringe benefits, shutting factories, abandoning communities, avoiding taxes, resisting environmental protections, and (in some cases) even rejecting the very idea of global warming.

Needless to say, the combined result has been transformative. American workers have seen a dramatic decline in their standard of living and quality of life (and economic security) since the 1980s. Meanwhile, 95 percent of the increase in personal incomes in recent years has gone to the top 1 percent of earners. The top 10 percent now take home about half the total national income and own 89 percent of all publicly traded stocks. Compensation for CEOs has also ballooned. In the 1940s, CEOs averaged some 20–40 times more income than their workers. These days, it is 250–350 times, or more.

Shareholder capitalism justifies its favoritism by claiming that, in the end, everyone will benefit from economic growth. In the modernized version of Adam Smith's "invisible hand" metaphor, it is said that a rising tide will lift all boats. The problem is that many of the boats have holes in their hulls and are bailing furiously to stay afloat, while the boats in the bottom quintile economically are actually sinking. It is a nautical disaster.

This situation, as well as our growing environmental crisis, have reignited the idea of returning to the more socially responsible model of "stakeholder capitalism." It would still provide rewards for merit, but this must be subordinated to serving the common good. Indeed, stakeholder capitalism has recently become a hot topic in academic journals and in the media. Most significantly, perhaps, the influential Business Roundtable released a statement in mid-2019, endorsed by nearly 200 US leading corporate CEOs, that called for a shift from shareholder capitalism to a "fundamental commitment to all of our stakeholders."

Although some large corporations nowadays have been voluntarily taking steps to become more stakeholder friendly, the greater challenge, as many observers have noted, is how to make this work more broadly and effectively. How do you engineer a change in the management values and boardroom behavior of a large company in a highly competitive marketplace without undermining its efficiency, flexibility, and profits – not to mention its stock price? Perhaps they should heed the advice of business leader Marc Benioff, the founder of the hugely successful company, Salesforce: "Skeptical business leaders who say having a purpose beyond profit hurts the bottom line should look at the facts. Research shows that companies which embrace a broader mission ... outperform their peers, grow faster, and deliver higher profits" (Benioff, 2018). (I will have more to say about this issue in Section 6.)

The third vitally important fairness precept (in addition to *equality* and *equity*) is *reciprocity*. Reciprocity is enshrined in the Golden Rule, and it lies at the ethical core of every major religion and every culture. When a disciple of Confucius asked him, "Is there any one word that could guide a person throughout life?," Confucius answered, "reciprocity. Never impose on others what you would not choose for yourself."

Reciprocity is also a practical necessity. For a start, it underlies the basic "exchange" principle in economic markets. More important, reciprocity is essential to sustaining the superorganism and providing for the basic needs of its members. We must all contribute a fair share in return for the benefits we receive, for no society can long exist on a diet of pure altruism – or with gaping budget deficits. Altruism is a means to a limited end (helping those in genuine need), not an end in itself.

Everyone who benefits from the superorganism has a reciprocal obligation to help support it, insofar as they can. This includes both the "makers" and the "takers" (to use Ayn Rand's egregious terminology) If the dirt-poor borrowers from the Grameen Bank (millions of small-scale "makers") are exemplary in repaying their loans, then our billionaires must also fully reciprocate for the benefits they receive from society. Otherwise, they are, in effect, free-riders on the rest of us; they are "takers." Indeed, there should be a special moral stigma attached to excessive wealth when it becomes a cause of harm to others and to the superorganism. And the fact is that the world is currently falling very far short of having access to the resources that will be needed to cope with our environmental crisis, much less providing for the basic needs of those who are, even now, living in extreme poverty or suffering from climate disasters and civil disorders of various kinds. A recent in-depth study at the University of Leeds (along with several collaborators) gathered extensive economic data for 150 countries and drew this overall conclusion: "No country in the world currently meets the basic needs of its citizens at a globally sustainable level of resources use" (Fanning et al., 2022: 26). Going forward, we will need to step up our game in terms of reciprocity and the common good, as we shall see in the final section.

The key to dealing with the life-threatening challenges we now face will be collective self-governance for the common good. In contrast with, say, the instinct-based system of the leaf-cutter ants, the human superorganism is based on social contracts among autonomous individuals, families, organizations, and governments. Our political leadership and governance processes depend on consent (and policing, of course). The whole–parts relationship is far more complicated, but it is clearly not impossible to get it right. Some positive examples will be described in the final section. In many cases, however, our governance systems must be improved; we are still on the learning curve as a species. We will need to reform and upgrade our corrupt and dysfunctional governments and build a comprehensive governance structure for our emerging global superorganism. We will also need to have governments at all levels that are devoted to the ancient principle of the "public trust" (more on all this as well in the final section).

If all these proposed changes turn out to be only "wishful thinking," "a pipe dream," "pie in the sky," or "a bridge too far" (choose your metaphor), then our species may well be doomed. Our inertia could amount to a suicide pact disguised as political "realism." We cannot afford to indulge in this kind of defeatism or in a nihilistic pessimism. To repeat, we must think outside the box, because our future lies outside the box. More important, we must act outside the box. Transformative social, economic, and political changes will be needed.

So, what will these changes look like, and how can we get from here to there?

6 The Next "Major Transition" in Evolution

Let's begin with a bookend for the dark future scenario that was described in Section 1. It offers us a more hopeful vision of our future.

The megadrought that has ravaged the southwestern portion of the United States is now in its fifteenth year. Although it has been hugely disruptive, the region has thus far been able to cope with it successfully. The economy has been severely damaged, but cooperation has been the overwhelming response. Citizens, private organizations, and governments at all levels have been able to coordinate their remedial efforts. This is due, in no small part, to the massive support and leadership provided by two new UN superagencies that were created under the comprehensive Global Governance Initiative in 2024.

Early on in the drought, the UN's new Global Infrastructure Fund (GIF) had designated the region as a high-risk area and had begun construction of twenty seawater desalination plants along the coastline under the new Global Social Contract between the UN and each of its 193 member countries. This involved a cooperative effort between the UN and the United States, with shared construction costs. As a result, these state-of-the-art freshwater plants are now all coming online. A fleet of tanker trucks and railroad tank cars is carrying the water inland to where it is needed. Major water conservation projects were also initiated in the region, and many state-of-the-art wastewater recycling plants are also in service.

This important UN project has been coupled with a massive effort, shared by the GIF and US federal, state, and local governments, to convert the region completely to solar, wind, geothermal, and tidal power systems – thus accelerating a transition that was already well underway before the drought. These new sources of clean electric power have also facilitated a near total conversion to electric cars, trucks, and buses.

As soon as it became clear that the drought was going to be prolonged and would produce an economic crisis across the region, the UN's new Global Emergency Management Agency (GEM) also stepped in and began a coordinated effort to minimize the damage (complete with a joint regional command center that included representatives from the affected states and organizations). The sweeping emergency measures that were imposed resemble how the United States mobilized to fight World War Two, even borrowing some of the same methods that were used back then. There has been strict food, water, and electric power rationing, along with price controls to prevent gaming the system. The potential for the emergence of a black market has also been strictly policed and punished. (It is the only fair alternative to relying on "market forces," or price inflation, which favors those with money and penalizes the poor.)

The severe constraints on business activity – from garden stores to lawn-care services, car washes, and restaurants – have been offset by various public employment programs, along with subsidized jobs for hard-pressed private sector employers that provide services like sanitation, transportation, hospitals, and hospices. Local mass transit systems have also been upgraded. The ailing economy has been helped by several measures that were enacted by a progressive, reform-minded US government after the 2024 election – a brand new Public

Service Employment program (PSE) that provides guaranteed jobs at a living wage whenever there is severe slack in the economy and an enhanced Affordable Care Act that provides universal, low-cost health care insurance, along with a new national homeless support program and an expanded food stamps, or SNAP, program. This has been coupled with a program to underwrite and assist with the relocation of idled workers and their families to other parts of the region, or the nation, wherever possible. Another important measure is a program designed to prevent mortgage foreclosures during these hard times, ranging from the use of home equity to cover payments (reverse mortgages) to equity sharing arrangements, and even some low-interest federal loans where appropriate.

Especially important is the GIF initiative to offset the crippling effects of the drought on large commercial farms across the region by creating some five million small backyard microfarms (based on multiples of 100 square-foot growing beds) using a highly productive organic growing method known as "biointensive." The biointensive system was developed in the twentieth century especially for third-world nations and small subsistence farms, and there were about seven million of them all told in over thirty countries as of 2018. Among its many advantages, the biointensive method can yield from two to six times more produce per acre (sometimes even more) than the typical commercial farm. It requires far less capital because it is labor intensive and uses simple hand tools that require only modest skills. Equally important, it uses 70–80 percent less irrigation water than the typical commercial farm, and it relies on compost grown in the garden itself for fertilizer. It can even build new topsoil over time if done properly. (Our own family used this method successfully for nearly a decade in the early 2000s on our sixteen-acre, four-season organic market farm on San Juan Island, Washington.)

You get the idea. A broad cooperative response, backed by major financial resources and relying on a combination of local citizen efforts, responsible stakeholder capitalism and government at all levels (including new UN agencies that are oriented to serving the common good rather than relying exclusively on capitalist "market solutions") is the only sure way to avoid a war of "each against all." As the billionaire Microsoft founder and philanthropist Bill Gates once put it in a TV interview, "markets only work for people who have money."

In the current political climate of resurgent nationalism and (very often) antagonistic relationships between nations, as well as skepticism about the shortcomings of the UN and even the very idea of adding more government, I would propose a two-step approach. At the start, there would be a strictly voluntary mutual aid agreement, along the lines of the 2015 Paris Climate

Accord and the 2021 and 2022 updates, that would assemble a pool of donated financial resources earmarked for assisting with major climate-related crises. This would be administered by existing UN agencies.

A model for how this might work is the successful Yakima River Basin "Integrated Plan" in the state of Washington, where several stakeholders have faced shrinking water supplies over time due to population increases, agricultural growth, climate change (especially droughts), and Native American fishing rights. After years of intractable conflict, the stakeholders came together around the principles of equitably shared sacrifices, plus the use of innovative efforts to mitigate the problems – for instance, by adding concrete linings to irrigation canals to minimize water losses, recycling and reusing water, and supplementing or replacing dams with fish ladders to accommodate the Yakima Indian fishermen. Above all, this was a cooperative solution, with shared benefits and shared costs.

However, I believe our ultimate response must be far more ambitious and comprehensive. Because we are now facing massive and prolonged environmental challenges that most countries cannot cope with alone (especially if they start preparing for them only after the disaster has occurred), we must act collectively to build a sustainable global superorganism – or else. Ideally, we should mobilize the necessary resources, management systems, organizational capabilities, and trained workers before these crises occur, and we must have an "all hands man your battle stations" response when they do.

The idea of "world government" is, of course, hardly new. It is an enduring dream that can be traced back at least to Bronze Age Egypt and the ancient Chinese emperors. In the modern era, it has been espoused by a great many prominent people, from Immanuel Kant to Albert Einstein, Winston Churchill, and Martin Luther King. Both the League of Nations and the UN, despite their limitations, were incremental steps in this direction. In the years after World War Two, the World Federalist Movement championed a more inclusive and powerful global regime. However, in recent decades the traditional idea of a top-down world government has largely been replaced by a more complex, polycentric, democratic vision of "global governance" – a global system of limited self-governing regimes and cooperative action with respect to specific transnational problems and domains, rather than an overarching, unified, all-powerful political authority.

As noted earlier, a significant degree of global governance of this nature has already evolved piecemeal over time in various specialized areas – international law, the law of the sea, international aviation, world trade, and more. There are also various academic institutes and a large body of research and publications that are now devoted to this subject, as well as a political globalization movement that includes such prominent theorists as Hazel Henderson, Fritjof Capra, Elisabet Sahtouris, Peter Russell, Herman Daly, Alvin and Heidi Toffler, Barbara Marx Hubbard, and others. But what has long been an aspiration has now become an imperative. As a recent review concluded: "Among different fields of global governance, environmental management is the most wanting in urgent answers to the crisis in the form of collective action by the whole human community" (Bennett & Satterfield, 2018). I believe we need both expanded global governance with respect to climate change and other urgent environmental and health problems, and an enhanced role for world government.

6.1 Global Governance Initiative

Here is my take on what this regime might look like (it should be considered a "draft" that is likely to be modified as these ideas are vetted and improved upon by others). What I am calling a Global Governance Initiative is grounded in the belief that there must be a major change in the dynamics of global politics and in the relationships between nations. A significant course change will be needed to meet our environmental crisis. Our system of deeply competitive nation-states must shift gears and become much more cooperative. The conflicts of interest and sometimes bitter animosities that now exist between various countries must be subordinated to a collective mission with shared benefits and costs. New financial resources and new organizational capabilities will also be required to stand up to these hurricane-force headwinds.

To reiterate some of the key points from Section 1, the greatest threat we may face is each other, and a regression into tribalism and violent conflict. Collective violence (warfare) has been one of the major themes in human history, going as far back as the evidence takes us. We are now facing the very real prospect of an era of terrorism and "climate wars." Or worse. Equally important, the challenges we face going forward will very often transcend national borders – from megadroughts to lethal disease pandemics and the growing horde of climate refugees. These crises will overwhelm the ability of many countries to deal with them unaided. A concerted international effort will be necessary. The basic idea is to create an overlay of new global services and support functions (backed by new financial resources) that are linked to a set of negotiated social contracts with each country, rather than trying to supplant them or deny their sovereign autonomy and impose solutions. In other words, the overall strategy would be to expand the scope and capabilities of existing international institutions, along with added political constraints and reforms in some countries, in return for an array of positive benefits. Call it the Edmund Burke, incremental reform model (see Section 3), or the big carrot, small stick strategy.

Before elaborating on this idea, there is an obvious prior question. How do we get from here to there? What we are talking about is a major shift in global politics and governance. There must be a change of "hearts and minds" at all levels within and between the world's deeply divided nations, especially the leaders and influential citizens in our most powerful countries. They must come to see that it is in their own self-interest, as well as an urgent moral imperative, to lead the way forward to a new global social contract and a collective effort to deal with the challenges we face.

Although we are currently a long way from such a consensus, there are some hopeful signs. One is the rising groundswell of volunteer organizing and grass-roots support for a greater effort to fight climate change. The pledges made by the many nations represented at the UN's COP15 and COP27 conferences in 2022 were also encouraging. In the United States, the outcome of the 2020 and 2022 mid-term elections were promising developments. The environment and climate change are now on the political agenda, at least. As I write this, the US President, Joe Biden, has reentered the Paris climate agreement and is strongly supporting measures to fight climate change. A growing number of businesses and prominent individuals are also responding in various ways.

But this is at best only a beginning. In his important new book, *Upheaval*, Jared Diamond (2019) provides several case studies of national crises where a major course change was achieved, and these can provide us with instructive models for the global crisis we face today. Among other things, there must be a broad public consensus that a crisis exists and that something must be done about it. There must be a general readiness to make major changes. There must be political initiative and a willingness to take responsibility for responding to the threat. There must be a clearly defined goal and a practicable solution. And there must be competent and skilled leadership to inspire and implement the necessary changes.

Historians and social scientists have long debated the question of which plays a more important role in social change: Is it "bottom-up" public pressure from ordinary citizens or "top-down" political leadership? Recent research suggests that the answer is both. Some of the most successful examples of major social changes and crisis responses have involved a synergistic combination of both "bottom-up" political movements (with strong public support) and effective "top-down" leadership. Each one empowers and informs the other, and neither one would have succeeded alone.

Everyone's favorite example is America's entry into World War Two. For several years after the outbreak of the war in Asia and Europe, America remained a deeply isolationist nation that seemed bent on avoiding involvement in the growing international carnage. This changed literally overnight after the surprise Japanese air attack on the Pacific fleet at Pearl Harbor on December 7, 1941. As the Japanese fleet admiral at the time (Isoroku Yamamoto) sadly commented afterward, the air assault had "awakened a sleeping giant." There was an immediate shift in public opinion and a broad consensus emerged for going to war. However, the country's response was also affected by public confidence in the government and a strong and capable leader, President Franklin Roosevelt, who had been quietly preparing for the war for several years. (For instance, the keels for all but one of the twenty-five first-line aircraft carriers built during the war were laid before the end of 1941.) After a rocky start early in 1942, Roosevelt and his military leaders were able to mount a highly effective global war effort.

It's now Pearl Harbor Day for our environmental crisis, but there may not be any psychological equivalent of the Pearl Harbor attack to catalyze our resolve. Instead, we may have to rely on the alternative model provided by the likes of the women's suffrage amendment in the early twentieth century and the civil rights legislation in the 1960s, where grassroots political movements inspired by effective leaders gradually won converts and built political support until, finally, the economic and political establishment got the message and acceded to major political reforms. A similar process of education and consensus building (nudged by the increasing frequency of climate-related natural disasters) may be our best hope for avoiding the metaphorical hangman's noose that I mentioned in Section 1. To paraphrase Samuel Johnson's famous line, nothing concentrates the mind like the prospect of being hanged in the morning. It is time for us all to look ahead and concentrate our minds on this life-and-death challenge.

Perhaps the most crucial missing piece at this point is global leadership. As our emerging environmental crisis intensifies, there will be no lack of doomsday demagogues – political con men who will try to exploit the situation to advance their personal agendas. Or ruthless nationalists who will pander to our ancient tribal instincts. This could well be the road to disaster for our species. What we desperately need is visionary "statesmen." In *The Republic*, Plato (1946/ 380 BC) stressed the central importance to any successful society of a leader who is devoted to acting in the public interest. A commitment to social justice is essential. Beyond this, an effective leader must have deep knowledge, wide experience, and the wisdom to use it effectively. And he/she must always tell the truth to the public. Anything less is a betrayal.

For the kind of change agent that we need to lead us to a new global super-organism, I would add to Plato's job description the ability to inspire, energize, and organize a massive collective effort. A great leader must also be a great communicator and a great administrator. In the twentieth century, I can think of the likes of Theodore Roosevelt, Winston Churchill, Franklin Roosevelt, John Kennedy, and, of course, Martin Luther King – whose dream of racial equality endures and still inspires.

Assuming, then, that widespread public support, an elite consensus, and inspired leadership ultimately emerges for taking collective action, it might then be possible to imagine a comprehensive package of amendments to the UN Charter – a "Global Governance Initiative" that would have to be approved by the Security Council (it would obviously have to include the United States, China, and Russia, among others) and by the necessary two-thirds of representatives to the General Assembly and its 193 member nations. This initiative should include, among other things: (1) a larger role for the UN itself in global governance and peacekeeping, along with the ability to intervene and help reform dysfunctional nation-state governments where needed; (2) a massive effort to deal with the growing freshwater shortages in many countries; (3) a global program to expand and diversify our fragile food production systems and adapt them to major climate disruptions; (4) supercharging the transition to clean, nonpolluting energy systems, along with providing low-cost electric power for the many underserved areas of the world; (5) a broad effort, focused especially on the developing countries, to build out a modern infrastructure for servicing a universal basic needs guarantee; and, finally, (6) a new UN superagency with the resources and capabilities needed to intervene and assist with severe climate emergencies.

Needless to say, a prerequisite for everything else on this to-do list is effective governance for the common good. This is, in fact, an age-old and enduring problem. It was first addressed by Plato in *The Republic*. As Plato expressed it, how do you control the controllers? His solution was to create a class of "guardians" that would carefully nurture and train philosopher kings, who would then selflessly devote themselves to ruling in the public interest. To his everlasting credit, Plato himself came to recognize that his vision was an unattainable ideal and in his last essay, the *Laws*, he proposed what he called a second-best alternative – "mixed" governments where all the major interests and classes are empowered and represented but also constrained by the rule of law. Although we have added many institutional elements to this vision over the past two millennia – from formal written constitutions (with "checks and balances," in the American model) to individual bills of rights, elections, legislatures, an independent judiciary, a free press, and more – Plato's second-best alternative remains the basic model for all modern democracies. As Winston Churchill wryly remarked, democracy is the very worst form of government, except for all the others.

These core principles of democratic self-government and the rule of law must also be applied to any expansion in the UN's global governance role. The UN must be an instrument for attaining the common good, not a power play in the coliseum of global politics.

There have been no less than five amendments to the basic UN Charter since 1945, along with many other proposals for reforms and improvements over the years. There have also been repeated efforts within the UN itself to improve the efficiency and effectiveness of the organization, and there are even satellite organizations dedicated to advancing a variety of UN reforms. Some proposals involve better ways for the UN to help resolve lethal conflicts. Others would streamline the bureaucracy of the UN Secretariat, or improve the organization's financing, or introduce more democracy, or consolidate the UN's diverse development programs. There is even a proposal for a separate, democratically elected "People's Assembly." (As an aside, the idea of creating a World Environmental Organization, or WEO, has also been on the table for more than thirty years.)

In this spirit, the Global Governance Initiative should, among other things, seek to enhance the executive and administrative authority of the UN and of the Secretary-General. After a transition period, it might also be possible for the Secretary-General to be popularly elected by exploiting the emerging global potential for interactive democracy and electronic voting (e-voting) – perhaps with candidates nominated by the Security Council. However, the Secretary-General should always be subject to recall by the Security Council and the General Assembly as a hedge against having a dysfunctional leader coupled with the rigidities of having a fixed term of office. (It is not difficult to think of a precedent.)

The size of the Security Council might also be increased (say to twenty-five), to allow both for additional permanent members and for broader participation among the rotating members. The Security Council's veto power should also be replaced with an "extraordinary majority" principle for key measures (requiring, say, the support of at least one-quarter of Council members to block a proposal).

The General Assembly could also be upgraded and reformed. Under the existing principle of one nation one vote, there is much dissatisfaction with how the General Assembly often seems to serve as a debating forum and megaphone for the developing countries. With small countries accounting for two-thirds of the membership, it is possible for a two-thirds vote (required for major proposals) to be obtained by a coalition of countries that represent only 5 percent of the global population. Perhaps some form of weighted voting by population size should be developed, analogous to the US House of Representatives. In time, a system of elections should also be developed in member countries for General Assembly seats. There is a large scholarly literature on such matters.

Beyond these structural improvements, I believe the Global Governance Initiative should also create two new superagencies under the authority of the Secretary-General and with Security Council oversight. They would have the mandates and, equally important, the additional financial resources needed to address our mounting survival challenges. I have called the first new super-agency the Global Infrastructure Fund (GIF). It would be charged with four of the major tasks listed earlier in this subsection: accelerating the effort to fight global climate warming, addressing our acute freshwater shortages, expanding and diversifying food production, and building out a basic infrastructure in the nations where it is still lacking, or incomplete, in order to undergird a universal basic needs guarantee. The GIF agency would also integrate and serve as an umbrella for existing agencies like the UNEP, UNDP, FAO, WHO, WFP, and the new UN Green Climate Fund, while providing the resources needed to greatly expand their efforts. This new umbrella superagency would, of course, also work closely with national and local governments and the many important NGOs.

One of the highest priorities for the new GIF agency – beyond climate warming itself – would be to address the growing number of freshwater shortages in various countries, as well as in major water-stressed urban areas – from Cape Town to Tokyo and London. The World Bank (n.d.) estimates that some two billion people, even now, live where there is potential water scarcity. This number could double by 2050.

This problem is compounded by a major political complication – a global trend toward privatization of water resources (turning water into a marketable commodity) and various conflicts over the long-standing principle of water as a public good. Two recent books on the subject, both titled *Water Wars* (Ward, 2002; Shiva, 2016/2002), detail the many political battles that have been waged over this issue in recent years. A potential resolution might be found in a UN mandate that fresh water is a basic need that must be provided to everyone and that this must constrain private property rights, though it would not negate them. As a practical matter, a policy of using public water subsidies – like food stamps for food purchases – might be one way of achieving political compromises where necessary.

However, the problem of dealing with absolute water scarcities in many parts of the world – a much greater threat – must be dealt with in a more comprehensive way. Remedial steps should start with measures designed to use existing water resources more efficiently (and reduce sewage and pollution). Another urgent priority would be to create more water catchment and storage systems in countries that are subject to increasingly erratic monsoon rain seasons. Drilling new wells in various locations may also be practicable. But this will not be nearly enough. Another alternative is a new generation of wastewater recycling systems that have vast potential to use scarce water resources more efficiently. However, there must also be a massive, global effort to build desalination plants, powered by renewable energy systems.

Although the cost of desalination technology has been cut in half over the past decade or so, it is still relatively expensive compared with drawing river water, or tapping underground aquifers (digging wells), or creating catchment ponds. But when there is an absolute water scarcity and no lower cost option is available, desalinated water is now feasible, if relatively expensive. Indeed, the biggest capital costs (which can vary widely) may be for land acquisition, facility construction, a reliable power source, salt brine waste removal, and water distribution systems. A rough guesstimate of the average cost might be about US$100 million for a plant that could serve 300,000 people. Thus, to build 100 desalination plants around the 4,600-mile coastline of the Indian subcontinent – enough to cover much of India's looming water shortfall – the total cost might be US$100 billion. As noted earlier, a recent NASA study (done from space) determined that no less than twenty-one of the world's thirty-seven largest aquifers have been drastically depleted, so desalination plants will need to be built in many vulnerable areas – from Australia to Africa, the Middle East, and California. Large quantities of water reserves will also be needed to meet various short-term water emergencies.

Equally crucial, the new GIF agency will need to undertake a broad global effort to increase and diversify our agricultural output, in part to feed those who are already suffering from hunger and malnutrition but, equally important, to spread the risks and help create large food reserves for the inevitable shortages that lie ahead. Accordingly, one part of an enhanced agricultural development program under the GIF (beyond what other development agencies are already doing) would be to assist with creating perhaps 200 million low-cost, biointensive "minifarms" around the world. These local minifarms might employ as many as 500 million people and produce enough to feed the farmers, their families, and perhaps others as well.

In theory, the biointensive farming method could feed the entire world with far less of the key inputs that are required for commercial agriculture – land, capital, water, fossil fuels, and soil amendments. A graphic prepared by the longtime leader in the development of biointensive farming, John Jeavons (2017), shows that one acre of farmland can be used either to support one cow, or to produce forty gallons of ethanol for automotive gas tanks, or to feed up to twenty people plus food for the soil (compost) using biointensive farming. The choice is up to us. (A recent UN study found that three-quarters of all the world's existing farms are small – under 2.5 acres – and locally oriented. Large-scale commercial market farms are mostly devoted to feeding the population, and their livestock, in developed countries.)

The second part of a GIF agricultural development program would be to provide additional resources to help sustain and improve production on large-scale commercial farms –shifting more of them over to no-till agriculture, converting to low-flow, drip irrigation systems, expanding organic food production, reducing soil erosion and pollution, developing new drought-tolerant and heat-tolerant crops, and other measures, as detailed by Earth scientist David Montgomery (2017) in his book, *Growing a Revolution*. Much could also be accomplished with the many innovative private-sector food production initiatives and technologies that have mushroomed in recent years. Many of these are described by environmental journalist Amanda Little (2019) in her visionary book, *The Fate of Food*.

Equally important, the GIF agricultural initiative would seek to create and maintain vast stores of emergency food. In 2017, it was estimated that world food reserves amounted to only a seventy-four-day supply. This would not be enough even to survive something like another "year without a summer" (caused by the worldwide dust cloud that resulted from the eruption of Mount Tambora in 1815), much less coping with multiple, sustained regional droughts. Given how vulnerable our global food production system is to climate changes, every one of the world's farms is important, and we need to develop many more of them. The profit-oriented capitalist market system cannot meet the need unaided, and the war in Ukraine has exacerbated the problem.

Much of the new GIF agency's work would augment the many programs already in place under the initiative of the UN's 2015 "Sustainable Development Goals," an international effort to achieve some seventeen broad economic and social goals. However, it would have the broader objective of supporting a universal basic needs guarantee. The satisfaction of our basic needs depends on much more than income. It also crucially depends on an extensive array of goods, services, and infrastructure: food that is affordable, adequate clean freshwater supplies, low-cost electrical power, efficient sewage disposal, human waste removal and sanitation systems, public transportation, communications technologies, public health and reproductive services, public education, and more. Many countries are still woefully lagging in providing their citizens with an adequate basic needs infrastructure. For instance, a program in India to finally install many millions of toilets and modern waste removal systems across that huge country has been struggling. Urban areas that are experiencing increasing life-threatening heat waves will also need to install and operate millions of the new, more energy efficient air conditioners.

The other proposed new UN superagency would be charged with responding to the kind of large-scale, prolonged environmental crisis portrayed in Section 1, and discussed at the beginning of this section. Like FEMA, the new Global Emergency Management Agency (I prefer GEM as an acronym) must not only be able to cope with multiple environmental crises but have the capabilities for providing sustained, longer-term aid, assisting with major economic adjustments and even facilitating some population out-migrations. It would greatly expand the efforts of the existing UN High Commission for Refugees and the new International Organization for Migration. Needless to say, both of these proposed new UN superagencies would also have to work closely and cooperatively with the many existing nation-state agencies and NGOs that have convergent missions (see also Wray et al., 2018).

As for the cost of all this, a very rough estimate is that at least US$2 trillion dollars of public money will be needed (in addition to what has already been committed by governments and the private sector) for accelerating the effort to convert the world to solar, wind, and other nonpolluting power systems, and for mitigating a range of related environmental problems – especially in poor countries that do not have the financial means. A second US$2 trillion is the minimum required for addressing long-term food and water resource problems in various countries, under the GIF. Another US$2 trillion should be allocated for infrastructure projects. And an additional US$2 trillion (at least) should be used for initial underwriting of the GEM and its efforts to cope with environmental crises that are already happening and getting worse. Of course, these two new superagencies will also need ongoing funding. And all this would have to be supplemented with whatever individual countries can do for themselves.

So where will this US$8 trillion (and probably more) come from? To gain some perspective on the matter, consider this: total global personal wealth in 2018 was US$317 trillion, according to the annual Credit Suisse (2018) *Global Wealth Report*, with half of it being owned by the top 1 percent, or about 7.5 million people. About 1,500 of these wealth-holders are billionaires. Jeff Bezos of Amazon was ranked first, with more than US$140 billion in 2018. In addition, Forbes Magazine compiled an estimate (probably on the low side) in 2017 that over US$8 trillion of invisible wealth has been hidden away in anonymous "offshore" bank accounts (the Tax Justice Network puts the total much higher, at US$20–30 trillion). Some of this money is there for legitimate purposes, but the bulk of it consists of tax dodges and nest eggs for the rich, the famous, and the infamous (like corrupt politicians and criminal cartels) (see Zucman, 2015). Likewise, it is estimated that about half of the world's total annual income (about US$70 trillion) goes to the top 10 percent of income earners. Using US data for 2014 as an indicator, the top 1 percent averaged

$465,000 in gross income (before taxes), and the top 5 percent averaged $214,000. Or consider global military spending. According to an authoritative estimate by the Stockholm International Peace Research Institute (SIPRI), the total in 2018 was over US$1.7 trillion, with the United States alone spending roughly US$700 billion, or more than one-third of the total (SIPRI Yearbook, 2018).

An important part of what the global power elite and the ultrarich must agree to do is to allow the global community to use a larger share of the world's surplus wealth to sustain the collective survival enterprise and build out our global superorganism. Thus, there might be a graduated global "wealth tax" (above some threshold minimum income) to raise a "war chest" of US$8–10 trillion dollars. This might be complemented by a graduated income tax, or perhaps a financial transactions tax to support the ongoing operating expenses for an upgraded UN and its new superagencies. Collecting these taxes would, of course, present a major political and administrative challenge. Perhaps the World Bank's mission and role could be expanded as both a collector and distributor of the financial resources needed for the UN's enhanced mission.

What's in it for these wealthy "donors"? Apart from the satisfaction of knowing that they are helping to save the world and paying their fair share to help support the global survival enterprise (honoring the reciprocity principle), they would also benefit politically. It would certainly help to counteract the resentment and antagonism toward the ultrarich that have been aroused by the current extremes of wealth and global poverty. It is no longer enough for a billionaire to have his/her name on the wall of a college dormitory, or to sponsor an art museum. Indeed, it might mitigate some of the ambient guilt feelings these days among some of our one-percenters.

But more significant, the UN's comprehensive Global Governance Initiative might include a unique new feature. Inspired by Plato's *Republic*, the idea would be to create a "Guardians' Council" that would provide a vehicle for wealthy contributors to monitor how their money is being used and allow them to have an oversight role via regular reports to the Security Council and the General Assembly. Among other things, this would give the people who are paying the bulk of the bills a collective voice in how the money is being used. It is highly unorthodox, but I believe it deserves a look.

So, how would all this work in practice? How could this initiative be integrated into the existing global system of independent nation-states? The answer, in a nutshell, is that the UN would negotiate a set of bilateral contracts with each country. Money talks, and big money talks even louder, especially when it involves help with urgent matters of life and death. In return for the billions of new dollars that are likely to flow directly to many of these nations, while many others would benefit indirectly by (in effect) obtaining access to a priceless disaster insurance policy and increased political stability (and fewer climate refugees), each nation would be required to accept a set of conditions tailored to its own economic and political situation. Collectively, I refer to it as a Global Social Contract.

These individualized agreements might include such things as: granting authority for the UN to act within each nation for the purpose of adding new infrastructure and, as necessary, to provide emergency management services; a binding pledge to operate and properly maintain any new infrastructure that is installed by the UN; requirements for internal government reforms and strong anti-corruption measures (the cost of government corruption worldwide is estimated to be greater than US$1 trillion a year and is a major cause of failed states); establishing or restoring the rule of law and an independent judiciary in deeply corrupted countries; a commitment from each country to ensure a basic income for all its citizens; and improvements where necessary to each nation's economic safety net.

In some special cases, these social contracts might also include extraordinary provisions to rebuild failed states, purge corrupt regimes, suppress self-serving warlords, even facilitate birth control measures where desperately needed. The global epidemic of addictive drugs must also be brought under control – no small task. An enhanced UN peacekeeping role might also be needed, as well as increased authority (and resources) to help resolve intractable international conflicts like Russia versus Ukraine, Iran versus Saudi Arabia, Israel versus Palestine, India versus Pakistan, North Korea versus South Korea, and more.

Any contract without teeth is wishful thinking, especially one with some potentially coercive features. So, the Global Governance Initiative would need to have another major element – the ability to police and punish those who do not fulfill their obligations and those nations (and leaders) that do not fully comply with the provisions of their contracts. To this end, the International Criminal Police Organization (INTERPOL) could be significantly expanded and its powers augmented. Established in 1923 and headquartered in Lyon, France, with "bureaus" in many other countries and with a current staff of about 750 and a budget of 113 million euros, INTERPOL now provides strictly voluntary mutual assistance to other police departments in 100 member countries.

Under the Global Governance Initiative, INTERPOL could be brought under the direct authority of the UN, and given the power to conduct investigations, issue subpoenas, make arrests, and extradite global tax evaders and/or those who might be responsible for violating any nation's contractual obligations to the UN. These enhanced (but still limited) international police powers would also need to be supplemented with the legal infrastructure necessary for investigating and prosecuting violators, along with an augmented international court system. One possibility would be to expand the definition of "crimes against humanity" to include acts of cheating or corruption that cause serious harm and undermine the universal basic needs guarantee. Good government is not optional. It is vital to our survival, and it presents a formidable challenge. Corruption is very much like a cancer that can spread and destroy the superorganism.

In addition to new capabilities for the superorganism at the global level, many of the other "parts" at all levels also have a role to play. Individual countries and the private sector are not absolved from sharing the burdens. Thus, two other sets of institutional changes are also essential to achieving and sustaining the common good. One of these involves a sea change in the values and the conduct of governments at all levels, and in every country. Government cannot simply be a tool for preserving an elite and its wealth, or an arena for the clash of competing economic interests, or for enhancing "national security" in the strictly military sense. Or worse, a tool for reviving imperialist ambitions. First and foremost, it must be an instrument for pursuing the common good (our basic survival needs). This is a fiduciary responsibility that goes all the way back to our remote origins as a species.

It happens that the idea of a collective (governmental) responsibility for the common good has a sturdy foundation in the concept of the "public trust." The basic idea can be traced back to a category of Roman laws – *Jus publicum*, or public law – which (among other things) pertained to resources that were, "by the law of nature," viewed as the common property of all humankind, including the air, water, seas, and seashores (according to the Institutes of Justinian). In the Medieval period, the idea of common ownership also came to be associated with such things as public thoroughfares and common pastures for grazing livestock. The principle that government has a responsibility and a role in protecting the commons is also embedded in English and American common law.

In modern times, the public trust doctrine has had many practical applications in various countries. In the United States, the federal government and a number of states have used it to protect natural resources. The state of Washington, for instance, has mandated that all the fresh waters in the state are owned by it as a common resource. Conditional "water rights" permits are required in order to use fresh water for any large commercial purpose. There have also been many legislative applications of the public trust principle over the years. Important examples in the United States include the landmark National Environmental Policy Act (NEPA) in 1970, as well as the many federal laws over the years that have established some 60 national parks and 500 historic sites encompassing over 50 million acres.

The public trust doctrine is also now being used as a legal tool for fighting climate change and other environmental problems. For instance, in a bellwether case in 2013, the Pennsylvania Supreme Court found elements of that state's hydraulic fracturing legislation to be unconstitutional and in violation of the public trust. Another important application of the public trust doctrine can be found in the so-called sovereign wealth funds, like Norway's huge nest egg. These publicly managed funds are authorized to hold and invest discretionary state revenues, such as royalties from the sale of crude oil, in ways that are intended to benefit the common good.

However, there is a deeper and broader interpretation of the public trust, championed by a number of legal scholars and some courts, which provides an opportunity for expanding its scope and application. The basic idea is that the public trust is a fundamental attribute of sovereignty in a democratic society – a "constitutive principle." It involves an inherent power to serve the public interest, and it has supremacy over contrary laws or individual property rights. As the University of Oregon law professor and public trust specialist Mary Christina Wood (2014: 132) observes in her book, *Nature's Trust*, "characterizing the trust as an attribute of sovereignty bores down to legal bedrock." In this interpretation, the public trust power and the ability to act in the public interest does not need to be backed by specific constitutional language or statutes. It no more needs to be spelled out than the police power, which is assumed to be a necessary element of sovereignty. Some legal scholars also contend that this obligation should not even be limited to the current generation. In Professor Wood's (2014: 126) words: "The core purpose of the public trust lies in protecting the citizens' unyielding interest in their own survival (and that of their children)."

It is, therefore, both logical and appropriate to conclude that the public trust encompasses whatever is required to sustain and advance the collective survival enterprise – the superorganism. All governments have a fiduciary responsibility to undergird and support the right to life and its indispensable corollary, a universal basic needs guarantee. Equally important, governments must impose a restraining and guiding influence on the private sector for the sake of the common good, or the public interest, including the interests of posterity. We are obviously very far from achieving these goals, but it is a target with a clearly defined bull's-eye; it is not some nebulous ideal (see P. G. Brown, 1994; Wilson, 2012, 2016).

One obvious priority is the imposition of a long-overdue carbon tax in various countries as a major incentive to discourage the use of fossil fuels and encourage private investment in renewable energy systems (though it must also try to avoid burdening the poor). The "price signal" of a carbon tax would help, but there is much more that both the public and the private sectors can and must do. Another promising idea is to recapture (or "sequester") large quantities of atmospheric CO_2 in the soil through improved farming practices. Reforestation – planting many more trees to convert CO_2 into oxygen – may also be beneficial.

In his deeply disturbing book, *This Is How the World Ends*, Jeff Nesbit (2018) estimates that it will require a staggering investment of about US\$99 trillion (roughly the equivalent of current total global GDP) to convert the world to renewable energy and transportation systems. However, a more hopeful vision can be found in the book, *Drawdown*, edited by Paul Hawken (2017). It is the product of a combined effort by some 200 scientists and researchers, world-wide, and it represents by far the most comprehensive and thoroughly vetted plan to date for coping with climate warming. It proposes some eighty specific changes, utilizing currently available technology, across various domains – energy, food, water, buildings, urban environments, transportation, materials, and more – as well as calling out more than twenty promising future technologies – from smart highways to microbial farming. Almost all of these measures would also produce jobs, improve public health, reduce pollution, restore the land, and save money. The overall cost would be huge, with an estimated total of more than US\$27 trillion. However, this would be offset by potential cost savings that might be as much as US\$74 trillion. Hawken calls them "no regrets" solutions. More important, in combination they would drastically reduce climate warming.

Much of this, or any plan to fight climate warming, must be executed by the private sector in various countries, and this brings us back to the concept of "stakeholder capitalism" – the other broad institutional change that is increasingly urgent. This is not primarily a matter of imposing additional regulations on private businesses (although some are certainly necessary; they establish the boundaries of the playing field and level it for the players). It is primarily about a change of "hearts and minds" – and the operative values – in our capitalist system. To repeat, the basic idea is that everyone who has an interest, or stake, in a business firm – managers, workers, subcontractors, suppliers, customers, governments, society, and, of course, the shareholders – should have an influence on its governance and behavior, and receive a fair share of the benefits.

The case for stakeholder capitalism is very strong (see Allen et al., 2007). For one thing, the claim that the shareholders deserve to take precedence because they are the "owners" of any publicly traded company is flatly contradicted by 200 years of legal theory, laws, and court rulings that define a corporation as an "autonomous individual" that owns itself. Nor are the shareholders favored in any (known) corporate charters. In fact, corporate managers and boards of directors have an explicit responsibility to pursue the well-being of a company as a separate entity. The shareholders have a legal claim only to the "residual value" of the company after all its other obligations are paid. Shareholders are not even the primary source of capital in corporate America these days. Much of it comes from debt financing.

It should also be pointed out that the workers are at much greater risk (including their livelihoods, their training, and their roots in a given community) than are the shareholders in an age when the duration of the average stockholding is about six months. A bias toward shareholders over other stakeholders is also at odds with every modern theory about how to manage people, going back to the work of management guru Peter Drucker in the 1960s. Efficiency and productivity in any large organization is heavily dependent on "social capital" – trust, fair dealing, and reciprocity.

A comparison with the performance of corporations in countries that have ignored or rejected the shareholder model also refutes the claim that it is a superior system. Germany, for instance, has a long-standing corporate governance arrangement called "co-determination," where workers are by law required to occupy up to one-half of the seats on the board of directors (depending on the size of the company) and where there is also a strong government voice in corporate behavior. The result is that this actually increases corporate responsibility and cooperation, and it has contributed to the formidable reputation of large German business firms for being highly efficient and profitable.

A formal theoretical model (and analysis) developed by the well-known economist Franklin Allen and colleagues (2007) also lends support to the stakeholder model. They showed that an alignment of interests among various stakeholders is both attainable – depending on the circumstances – and that it can lead to higher overall efficiency and value for a firm. They cite a number of concrete examples in various countries, ranging from Germany and the Nordic countries to Japan, Austria, and Luxembourg. More recently, a new US study showed that American companies with narrower pay gaps between the CEO and the workers tend to perform better (Benioff & Langley, 2019). By the same token, there are now many thriving nonprofit business firms and organized cooperatives, as well as a relatively new category of so-called B-Corporations that are committed to pursuing values that are more aligned with the stakeholder model. (There are currently more than 550 B-Corporations, as well as 960 others that meet the certification standards.) Marc Benioff, the chairman and co-CEO of Salesforce, who was quoted in Section 5, stresses that "We don't have to choose between doing well and doing good" (Benioff & Langley, 2019).

One significant indicator that a sea change toward stakeholder capitalism may be possible is the recently created UN Global Compact, which, so far, includes some 9,500 companies in 160 countries that have pledged to strive for greater corporate responsibility and sustainability and to make annual public reports. The recent Business Roundtable endorsement of stakeholder capitalism was also significant. Another hopeful sign is the recent announcement by Laurence Fink, the CEO of BlackRock – by far the world's largest investment house (with some US$6.3 trillion under management) – that henceforth it would require its clients to be socially responsible. "Society is demanding that companies, both public and private, serve a social purpose," he wrote (Sorkin, 2018). In this spirit, Walmart – America's largest employer – recently announced that it would use some of its savings from the 2017 tax law to increase the minimum wage of its employees and it has begun to convert its 3,275 "supercenter" stores to solar power. Many other companies are doing as much or even more these days. We still have a long way to go. But, to borrow another punchline from Winston Churchill, it may at least be the end of the beginning.

Finally, it should be stressed that the idea of a society whose government and private sector are oriented to serving the common good is not just hypothetical, or an unattainable ideal. There are some real-world examples. What has been called the Nordic Model – including especially Norway, Denmark, Finland, and other Scandinavian countries – encompasses full employment at decent wages, a relatively flat distribution of income, a full array of supportive social welfare services, extensive investment in infrastructure, excellent free education and health care, a generous retirement system, high social trust, a strong commitment to democracy, and a government that is sensitive to the common good, not to mention having a competitive capitalist economy (yes, capitalist) with high productivity and deep respect for the environment. (These countries consistently rank at the top in international surveys of human development and happiness.) To top it off, Norway's sovereign wealth fund currently totals more than US$1 trillion, a huge nest egg for such a small country. (See Partanen, 2016.)

Some apologists for American-style capitalism are dismissive about Norway, viewing it as an exception because it has the advantage of all those North Sea oil profits. Yes, but, America was endowed with vastly greater oil deposits, which it has been exploiting for over 100 years. So where is its sovereign wealth fund? Why is its social safety net so badly frayed and its infrastructure deteriorating?

Communism sought to abolish private property in the "means of production." In contrast, the public trust doctrine and stakeholder capitalism would respect the contributions of capitalism and honor the important fairness principle of equity, or rewards for merit. However, it would also impose limits, and constraints, and, more important, subordinate our global capitalist system to the common good – starting with climate change. Capitalism must be a servant of the superorganism, not the other way around. To reiterate, the right to life takes precedence over property rights. This must be a foundational moral principle.

Beyond the few outstanding real-world examples like the Scandinavian countries, the challenge of realizing a global society dedicated to the common good and a universal basic needs guarantee – not to mention governments devoted to the public trust – is a daunting task, to say the least. When physicist Albert Einstein was once asked why we were smart enough to produce atomic energy but could not contain nuclear weapons and the arms race, he answered: "It is because politics is more difficult than physics." (To this I would add that people are much more complicated than quarks.)

The journalist James Traub (2018), in a remembrance for the late UN Secretary-General Kofi Annan, mourned what he called Annan's "tragic idealism." He concluded: "Surely the greatest tribute to Kofi Annan's legacy would be to act in such a way as to make the United Nations the kind of force that he, and so many of us, wish that it were. Maybe that day will come – but not any time soon." I believe that this is not good enough. To reiterate Tom Friedman's punch line, "later will be too late."

Our global superorganism desperately needs a global system of governance that is devoted to the common good. It is literally a matter of life and death. However, the next major transition in evolution cannot be imposed from the top down. The changes we need must begin with changing hearts and minds at all levels. A "legitimate" world government will arise as an organic, "polycentric" process, in political scientist Elinor Ostrom's (2009, 2015) formulation, with both bottom-up and top-down reforms and innovations. There must be a "Green New Deal" in every country – or perhaps a "Green Real Deal," to borrow a slogan that was coined for California's financially and politically more attractive plan. Everyone must climb aboard this speeding train, and we must act collectively to alter its course before we plunge over the cliff. No single one of the changes and reforms I have outlined here will achieve this goal. It will require an enormous cooperative effort, complete with new values and transcendent new forms of synergy. And, of course, there will be an immense number of devilish details to be worked out, not to mention managing the politics.

Is all this an unattainable ideal? The answer, I believe, is that we have no viable alternative. Idealism at its best is not about wishful thinking. Innovation is the very essence of what we are as a species, and ideals are the fathers (and mothers) of social and political change. Our ideals can inspire and empower the actions needed to achieve our goals. (Again, think of women's suffrage, social security, civil rights, or the growing climate action movement, not to mention all those social reforms in nineteenth-century Great Britain.) If you have a vision of a better world, and if you stand up and fight for it, you may be able to turn pessimism into hope, and active hope is the fuel that powers social change. And if the result is only half a loaf, that is a good start; it may also whet our appetites for more.

There is a spreading mood of gloom in various quarters nowadays about the environmental crisis. I call it the "doomsday caucus." It includes a significant number of the world's leading scientists, as well as many mainstream environmental experts, professional writers, political activists, and many others who have given up hope that there can be any technological, economic, or political fixes for global warming and our ecological "overshoot". To these pessimists, the apocalypse is already baked in. Anything we do now is too little, too late.

I believe that such defeatism in the face of our global life-and-death crisis represents a classic example of a self-fulfilling prophesy. There is a great deal more that can be done to mitigate potential future damage and prevent a full-scale ecological Armageddon. I believe that doing everything we can to cope with the crisis is far better than doing nothing. I much prefer the risk of failure to the certainty of failure.

In the end, our response to the undeniably hard and convulsive times that lie ahead is a matter of personal perspective, and temperament. It goes beyond the borders of any purely objective, rational analysis. It requires a vision. And active hope. And inspired leadership. As the youthful British Prime minister, William Pitt, told his wavering young friend and colleague William Wilberforce (in the recent movie, *Amazing Grace*, about the twenty-year struggle to abolish the slave trade in England), "We're too young to realize that certain things are impossible. So, we will do them anyway."

6.2 "We Must All Survive Together"

To sum up, then, we are confronting an unprecedented survival crisis, where even our worst-case scenarios may not be realistic enough. Menacing new climate-related disasters now seem to be an almost daily occurrence. Our survival problem clearly transcends and obliterates national boundaries. We are collectively in peril. Any "we vs. they" survival of the fittest response will likely be hugely costly and self-defeating, and we cannot depend on unfettered capitalism and "market forces" to solve our problems. As we have seen, when the have-nots are desperate and have nothing left to lose, they will do desperate things. And so too will desperate nations. We could all pay a terrible price for inaction.

The key to our evolutionary success as a species has always been cooperation, adaptive innovations, and synergy, and these must also define our path going forward. In order to respond effectively to the destructive challenges that lie ahead, we must mobilize a significant share of the world's surplus wealth and prepare for the future now, because the future is already well underway. We must also undergird everything we do with the Fair Society principles (*equality*, *equity*, and *reciprocity*), and we must make a collective commitment to a universal basic needs guarantee. Above all, we must have governance at all levels that is dedicated to the public trust, and a global economic system and private sector that serves the common good. Every part must do its bit for the collective survival enterprise – the superorganism. But there must be reciprocal benefits in return for all the stakeholders and contributors.

The very survival of our emerging global superorganism and its many parts must now become our overriding priority. To echo Benjamin Franklin once again, we must all survive together, or we will go extinct separately. It is time to concentrate our minds on the hangman's noose. Both our past and our future as a species – our ancient heritage and our ultimate fate – are calling on us to respond. It is Pearl Harbor Day. The time for us to choose is now. Later will be too late.

Bibliography

Abi-Habib, M. & Kumar, H. (2018). Deadly tensions rise as India's water supply runs dangerously low. *New York Times*, June 17, 2018.

Ackerman, B. & Alstott, A. (1999). *The Stakeholder Society*. New Haven, CT: Yale University Press.

Allen F., Carletti, E., & Marquez, R. (2007). Stakeholder capitalism, corporate governance and firm value. Wharton Financial Institutions Center Working Paper #09-28.

Allen, P. (1983). *Who Sank the Boat?* New York, NY: Coward-McCann.

Angier, N. (2018). A population that pollutes itself into extinction (and it's not us). *New York Times*, April 30.

Applebaum, A. (2020). *Twilight of Democracy: The Seductive Lure of Authoritarianism*. New York, NY: Penguin Random House.

Aristotle. (1946/ca. 350 BC). *Politics*. Oxford: Oxford University Press.

Aristotle. (1961/ca. 350 BC). *The Metaphysics*. Cambridge, MA: Harvard University Press.

Arnold, J. (Ed.) (2001). *The Origins of a Pacific Coast Chiefdom: The Chumash of the Channel Islands*. Salt Lake City: University of Utah Press.

Beinhocker, E. D. (2006). *The Origin of Wealth: Complexity and the Radical Remaking of Economics*. Boston, MA: Harvard Business School Press.

Bendell, J. (2018). Deep adaptation: a map for navigating climate tragedy. Institute of Leadership and Sustainability Occasional Paper 2, University of Cumbria, UK.

Benioff, M. (2018). We need a new capitalism. *New York Times*, October 14.

Benioff, M. & Langley, M. (2019). *Trailblazer: The Power of Business as the Greatest Platform for Change*. New York, NY: Random House.

Bennett, N. J. & Satterfield, T. (2018). Environmental governance: a practical framework to guide design, evaluation, and analysis. *Conservation Letters, A Journal of the Society for Conservation Biology* 11 (6): e12600. https://doi.org/10.1111/conl.12600.

Berg, J. (2018). Editorial, tomorrow's Earth. *Science* 360 (639): 1379. https://doi.org/10.1126/science.aau5515.

Boehm, C. (1999). *Hierarchy in the Forest: The Evolution of Egalitarian Behavior*. Cambridge, MA: Harvard University Press.

Boehm, S. & Schumer, C. (2023). 10 big findings from the 2023 IPCC report on climate change. World Resources Institute, March 20. www.wri.org/insights/2023-ipcc-ar6-synthesis-report-climate-change-findings.

Boers, N. & Rypdal, M. (2021). Critical slowing down suggests that the western Greenland ice sheet is close to a tipping point. *Proceedings of the National Academy of Sciences* 118 (21): e2024192118. https://doi.org/10.1073/pnas.2024192118.

Brandon, H. (1969). A talk with Walter Lippmann at 80, about this "minor dark age." *New York Times Magazine*, September 14, p. 25ff.

Bremmer, I. (2018). *Us vs. Them: The Failure of Globalism*. New York, NY: Portfolio/Penguin.

Brown, D. E. (1991). *Human Universals*. Philadelphia, PA: Temple University Press.

Brown, L. R. (2009). *Plan B 4.0: Mobilizing to Save Civilization*. New York, NY: W. W. Norton.

Brown, L. R. (2011). *World on the Edge: How to Prevent Environmental and Economic Collapse*. New York, NY: W. W. Norton.

Brown, P. G. (1994). *Restoring the Public Trust: A Fresh Vision for Progressive Government in America*. Boston, MA: Beacon Press.

Burke, E. (2021/1790). Reflections on the Revolution in France. In *Project Gutenberg eBook of the Works of the Right Honourable Edmund Burke*, Vol. 03 (of 12). www.gutenberg.org/cache/epub/15679/pg15679-images.html.

Burke, J. A. & Hamer, R.L. (Eds.). (1999). *The Works of Edmund Burke, Volume 2*. New York: Harper & Brothers.

Business Roundtable. (2019). *Principles of Corporate Governance*. Washington, DC.

Capra, F. & Luisi, P. L. (2014). *The Systems View of Life: A Unifying Vision*. Cambridge: Cambridge University Press.

Chaplin-Kramer, R., Sharp, R. P., Weil, C., et al. (2019). Global modeling of nature's contributions to people. *Science* 366: 255–258.

Chayes, S. (2015). *Thieves of State: Why Corruption Threatens Global Security*. New York, NY: W. W. Norton.

Chuang, Z. & Bing, L. (2017). Temperature increase reduces global yields of major crops in four independent estimates. *Proceedings of the National Academy of Sciences* (Agricultural Sciences) 114 (35): 9326–9331.

Clark, J. C. D. (Ed.). (2001). *Reflections on the Revolution in France: A Critical Edition*. Stanford, CA: Stanford University Press.

Cochran, G. & Harpending, H. (2009). *The 10,000 Year Explosion: How Civilization Accelerated Human Evolution*. New York, NY: Basic Books.

Conradt, L. & Roper, T. J. (2003). Group decision-making in animals. *Nature* 421: 155–158.

Corning, P. A. (1983). *The Synergism Hypothesis: A Theory of Progressive Evolution*. New York, NY: McGraw-Hill.

Corning, P. A. (2003). *Nature's Magic: Synergy in Evolution and the Fate of Humankind*. Cambridge: Cambridge University Press.

Corning, P. A. (2005). *Holistic Darwinism: Synergy, Cybernetics and the Bioeconomics of Evolution*. Chicago, IL: University of Chicago Press.

Corning, P. (2011). *The Fair Society: The Science of Human Nature and the Pursuit of Social Justice*. Chicago, IL: University of Chicago Press.

Corning, P. (2018). *Synergistic Selection: How Cooperation Has Shaped Evolution and the Rise of Humankind*. Singapore: World Scientific.

Corning, P. A. (2023a). Teleonomy in evolution: "The ghost in the machine." In Corning, P. A., Kauffman, S. A., Noble, D., et al. (Eds.), *Evolution "On Purpose": Teleonomy in Living Systems*. Cambridge, MA: MIT Press, pp. 11–33.

Corning, P. (2023b). Ayn Rand shrugged: Time to reject a dangerous doctrine. *PR for People, The Connector Magazine*, April 7.

Couzin, I. (2007). Collective minds. *Nature* 445: 715. https://doi.org/10.1038/445715a.

Credit Suisse. (2018). *Global Wealth Report*. https://bit.ly/3AoOp5j.

Dalin, C., Wada, Y., Kastner, T., & Puma, M. J. (2017). Groundwater depletion embedded in international food trade. *Nature 543*: 700–704. https://doi.org/10.1038/nature21403.

Darwin, C. H. (1874/1871). *The Descent of Man and Selection in Relation to Sex*. New York, NY: A. L. Burt.

Darwin, C. R. (1968/1859). *On the Origin of Species by Means of Natural Selection, or the Preservation of Favoured Races in the Struggle for Life*. Baltimore, MD: Penguin.

Dawkins, R. (1989/1976). *The Selfish Gene*. New York, NY: Oxford University Press.

Diamond, J. M. (2005). *Collapse: How Societies Choose to Fail or Succeed*. New York, NY: Viking.

Diamond, J. (2019). *Upheaval: Turning Points for Nations in Crisis*. New York, NY: Little, Brown and Company.

Ehrlich P. R. (1968). *The Population Bomb*. New York, NY: Ballantine.

Ehrlich, P. R. & Ehrlich, A. H. (2012). Can a collapse of global civilization be avoided? *Proceedings of the Royal Society B* 280: 2845. http://dx.doi.org/10.1098/rspb.2012.2845.

Ehrlich, P. R. & Harte, J. (2015). Opinion: To feed the world in 2050 will require a global revolution. *Proceedings of the National Academy of Sciences* 112: 14743–14744. https://doi.org/10.1073/pnas.1519841112.

Ellis, E. C. (2018). Science alone won't save the Earth. People have to do that. *New York Times*, August 11.

Fanning, A. L., O'Neill, D. W., Hickel, J., & Roux, N. (2022). The social shortfall and ecological overshoot of nations. *Nature Sustainability* 5: 26–36. https://doi.org/10.1038/s41893-021-00799-z.

FAO. (2021). *The State of Food Security and Nutrition in the World*. Rome: FAO. https://bit.ly/3L4tcUb.

FAO. (2022). Global Soil Partnership: Saving our soil by all earthly ways possible, July 29.

Felber, C. (2015). *Change Everything: Creating an Economy for the Common Good*. London: Zed books.

Flannery, K. & Marcus, J. (2012). *The Creation of Inequality: How Our Prehistoric Ancestors Set the Stage for Monarchy, Slavery, and Empire*. Cambridge, MA: Harvard University Press.

Flavelle, C. (2019). Climate change threatens the world's food supply, United Nations warns. *New York Times*, August 8.

Fleming, D. (2016). *Surviving the Future: Culture, Carnival and Capital in the Aftermath of the Market Economy*. White River, VT: Chelsea Green Publishing.

Frase, P. (2016). *Four Futures: Life After Capitalism*. Brooklyn, NY: Verso.

Frohlich, N. & Oppenheimer, J. A. (1992). *Choosing Justice: An Experimental Approach to Ethical Theory*. Berkeley: University of California Press.

Friedman, M. (1962). *Capitalism and Freedom*. Chicago, IL: University of Chicago Press.

Fukuyama, F. (1992). *The End of History and the Last Man*. New York, NY: Free Press.

Gare, A. (2017). *The Philosophical Foundations of Ecological Civilization: A Manifesto for the Future*. London: Routledge.

Gillespie, L. (2023). Bankrate's 2023 annual emergency savings report. Bankrate, February 23. www.bankrate.com/banking/savings/emergency-savings-report/.

Gowdy, J. M. (Ed.) 1998. *Limited Wants, Unlimited Means: A Reader on Hunter-Gatherer Economics and the Environment*. Washington, DC: Island Press.

Graeber, D. & Wengrow, D. (2021). *The Dawn of Everything: A New History of Humanity*. New York, NY: Farrar, Straus and Giroux.

Greer, J. M. (2016). *Dark Age America: Climate Change, Cultural Collapse, and the Hard Future Ahead*. Gabriola Island, BC: New Society Publishers.

Griggs, B. W., Sanderson, M. R., & Miller-Klugesherz, J. A. (2020). Farmers are depleting the Ogallala Aquifer because the government pays them to do it. *The Conversation*, November 9. https://bit.ly/3ogYm1Y.

Guram, F. V. S. (2022). Climate change drives down yields and nutrition of Indian crops. *The Third Pole*, July 14.

Guterres, A. (2023). Rising seas risk climate migration on "biblical scale," says U.N. chief. *Washington Post*, February 15.

Haberman, C. (2018). "This is not a drill": The threat of nuclear annihilation. *New York Times*, May 13.

Halpin, J., Agne, K., & Jain, N. (2021). Americans want the federal government to help people in need. Center for American Progress, March 10. www .americanprogress.org/article/americans-want-federal-government-help-people-need/.

Hansen, J. (2009). *Storms of My Grandchildren*. New York, NY: Bloomsbury.

Harari, Y. N. (2017). *Homo Deus: A Brief History of Tomorrow*. New York, NY: HarperCollins.

Hardin, G. (1968). The tragedy of the commons. *Science* 162: 1243–1248. https://doi.org/10.1126/science.162.3859.1243.

Hawken, P. (Ed.) (2017). *Drawdown: The Most Comprehensive Plan Ever Proposed to Reverse Global Warming*. New York, NY: Penguin.

Heinberg, R. (2011). *The End of Growth: Adapting to Our New Economic Reality*. Gabriola Island, BC: New Society Publishers.

Henderson, H. (1996). *Building a Win–Win World: Life Beyond Economic Warfare*. San Francisco, CA: Berrett-Koehler.

Henderson, H. (with Sethi, S.). (2006). *Ethical Markets: Growing the Green Economy*. White River Junction, VT: Chelsea Green Publishing.

Henrich, J. (2016). *The Secret of Our Success: How Culture Is Driving Human Evolution, Domesticating Our Species, and Making Us Smarter*. Princeton, NJ: Princeton University Press.

Heylighen, F. (2007). The global superorganism: An evolutionary-cybernetic model of the emerging network society. *Journal of Social and Evolutionary Systems* 6 (1): 58–119.

Hobbes, T. (2010/1651). *Leviathan*. Peterborough, Canada: Broadview Press.

Hölldobler, B. & Wilson, E. O. (2009). *The Superorganism: The Beauty, Elegance and Strangeness of Insect Societies*. New York, NY: W. W. Norton.

Inglehart, R. F. (2018). *Cultural Evolution: People's Motivations Are Changing and Reshaping the World*. Cambridge: Cambridge University Press.

Jeavons, J. (2017). *How to Grow More Vegetables (and Fruits, Nuts, Berries, Grains, and Other Crops) Than You Ever Thought Possible on Less Land with Less Water Than You Can Imagine* (9th ed.). Willits, CA: Ten Speed Press.

Kelly, G., Kelly, D., & Gamble, A. (Eds.) (1997). *Stakeholder Capitalism*. New York, NY: St. Martin's Press.

Kishore, N., Marqués, D., Mahmud, A., et al. (2018). Mortality in Puerto Rico After Hurricane Maria. *New England Journal of Medicine* 379: 162–170. www.nejm.org/doi/pdf/10.1056/NEJMsa1803972.

Korten, D. C. (2015a). *When Corporations Rule the World* (3rd ed.). Oakland, CA: Berrett-Koehler Publishers.

Korten, D. C. (2015b). *Change the Story, Change the Future: A Living Economy for a Living Earth.* Oakland, CA: Berrett-Koehler Publishers.

Le Maho, Y. (1977). The emperor penguin: A strategy to live and breed in the cold. *American Scientist* 65: 680–693.

Leahy, S. (2019). Billions face food, water shortages over the next 30 years as nature fails. *National Geographic*, October 10.

Leigh, E. G., Jr. (1983). When does the good of the group override the advantage of the individual? *Proceedings of the National Academy of Sciences* 80: 2985–2989. https://doi.org/10.1073/pnas.80.10.2985.

Leigh, E. G., Jr. (1991). Genes, bees and ecosystems: The evolution of a common interest among individuals. *Trends in Ecology and Evolution* 6: 257–262. https://doi.org/10.1016/0169-5347(91)90073-7.

Lenin, V. (1902). What Is to Be Done? *Iskra* 4: 347–530.

Little, A. (2019). *The Fate of Food: What We'll Eat in a Bigger, Hotter, Smarter World.* New York, NY: Harmony Books.

Locke, J. L. (1970/1690). *Two Treatises of Government* (P. Laslett, Ed.). Cambridge, MA: Harvard University Press.

Lu, D. & Flavelle, C. (2019). Rising seas will erase more cities by 2050, new research shows. *New York Times*, October 29.

Malthus, T. R. (2008/1798). *An Essay on the Principle of Population.* Oxford: Oxford World's Classics.

Margulis, L. & Fester, R. (Eds.) (1991). *Symbiosis as a Source of Evolutionary Innovation: Speciation and Morphogenesis.* Cambridge, MA: MIT Press.

Markham, L. (2018). A warming world creates desperate people. *New York Times*, June 29.

Maynard Smith, J. (1982). The evolution of social behavior – A classification of models. In King's College Sociobiology Group (Eds.), *Current Problems in Sociobiology.* Cambridge: Cambridge University Press, pp. 28–44.

Maynard Smith, J. & Szathmáry, E. (1995). *The Major Transitions in Evolution.* Oxford: Freeman Press.

Maynard Smith, J. & Szathmáry, E. (1999). *The Origins of Life: From the Birth of Life to the Origin of Language.* Oxford: Oxford University Press.

McKibbon, B. (2019). *Falter: Has the Human Game Begun to Play Itself Out?* New York, NY: Henry Holt and Company.

McKinsey Global Institute. (2017). *Jobs Lost, Jobs Gained: What the Future of Work Will Mean for Jobs, Skills and Wages.* https://bit.ly/40AYren.

Meadows, D., Randers, J., & Meadows, D. (2004). *Limits to Growth: The 30-Year Update.* White River Junction, VT: Chelsea Green Publishing.

Michod, R. E. (1999). *Darwinian Dynamics: Evolutionary Transitions in Fitness and Individuality*. Princeton, NJ: Princeton University Press.

Milius, S. (2017). Worries grow that climate change will quietly steal nutrients from major food crops. *Science News*, December 13. www.sciencenews.org/article/nutrition-climate-change-top-science-stories-2017-yir.

Monbiot, G. (2017). *Out of the Wreckage: A New Politics for an Age of Crisis*. London: Verso.

Montgomery, D. R. (2017). *Growing a Revolution: Bringing Our Soil Back to Life*. New York, NY: W. W. Norton.

Mooney, C. (2019). Scientists triple their estimates of the number of people threatened by rising seas. *Washington Post*, October 29.

Nesbit, J. (2018). *This Is the Way the World Ends: How Droughts and Die-offs, Heat Waves and Hurricanes Are Converging on America*. New York, NY: Thomas Dunne.

Nolan, C., Overpeck, J. T., Allen, J. R. M., et al. (2018). Past and future global transformation of terrestrial ecosystems under climate change. *Science* 361 (6405): 920–923. http://doi:10.1126/science.aan5360.

O'Neill, D., Fanning, A. L., Lamb, W. F., & Steinberger, J. K. (2018). A good life for all within planetary boundaries. *Nature Sustainability* 1: 88–95. https://doi.org/10.1038/s41893-018-0021-4.

Ostrom, E. (2009). A polycentric approach for coping with climate change. Policy Research Paper 5095. Washington, DC: The World Bank.

Ostrom, E. (2015). *Governing the Commons: The Evolution of Institutions for Collective Action*. New York, NY: Cambridge University Press.

Paine, T. (1791–2). *The Rights of Man*. Published as a pamphlet in two parts.

Partanen, A. (2016). *The Nordic Theory of Everything: In Search of a Better Life*. New York, NY HarperCollins.

Phelan, J. (2022). Italy's plan to save Venice from sinking. *BBC*, September 28. www.bbc.com/future/article/20220927-italys-plan-to-save-venice-from-sinking.

Pierre-Louis, K. (2018). Antarctica is melting three times as fast as a decade ago. *New York Times*, June 13.

Pinker, S. (2018). *Enlightenment Now: The Case for Reason, Science, Humanism, and Progress*. New York, NY: Penguin Group.

Plato. (1946/380 BC). *The Republic*. Cleveland, OH: World Publishing Company.

Polanyi, K. (2001/1944). *The Great Transformation: The Political and Economic Origins of Our Time*. Boston, MA: Beacon Press.

Porritt, J. (2005). *Capitalism: As If the World Matters*. London:Earthscan.

Price, R. (1789). *A Discourse on the Love of Our Country*. Speech and pamphlet.

Rand, A. (1943). *The Fountainhead.* New York, NY: Bobbs-Merrill.

Raworth, K. (2018). *Doughnut Economics: Seven Ways to Think Like a 21st-Century Economist.* White River Junction, VT: Chelsea Green Publishing.

Reich, R. B. (2018). *The Common Good.* New York, NY: Alfred A. Knopf.

Reiley, L. (2019). The new plan to remove a trillion tons of carbon dioxide from the atmosphere: Bury it. *Washington Post,* June 12.

Rich, N. (2019). *Losing Earth: A Recent History.* New York, NY: Farrar, Strauss and Giroux.

Rousseau, J-J. (1984/1762). *Of the Social Contract* (Trans. Charles M. Sherover). New York, NY: Harper & Row.

Sachs, J. D. (2006). *The End of Poverty: Economic Possibilities for Our Time.* New York, NY: Penguin.

Sachs, J. D. (2017). *Building the New American Economy: Smart, Fair & Sustainable.* New York, NY: Columbia University Press.

Sapolsky, R. M. (2017). *Behave: The Biology of Humans at Our Best and Worst.* New York, NY: Penguin Press.

Science News. (2015). Earth's groundwater reserves likely far smaller than thought, June 17.

Scranton, R. (2018). *We're Doomed. Now What? Essays on War and Climate Change.* New York, NY: Soho Press.

Seeley, T. D. (1995). *The Wisdom of the Hive: The Social Physiology of Honey Bee Colonies.* Cambridge, MA: Harvard University Press.

Seeley, T. D. (2010). *Honeybee Democracy.* Princeton, NJ: Princeton University Press.

Shiva, V. (2016/2002). *Water Wars: Privatization, Pollution, and Profit.* Berkeley, CA: North Atlantic Books.

SIPRI Yearbook. (2018). *Armanments, Disarmament and International Security.* www.sipri.org/yearbook/2018.

Skinner, B. F. (1981). Selection by consequences. *Science* 213 (4507): 501–504.

Smith, A. (1964/1776). *The Wealth of Nations* (2 Vols.). London: Dent.

Sorkin, A. R. (2018). Blackrock's message: Contribute to society or risk losing our support. *New York Times,* January 15.

Steffen, W., Rockström J., Richardson, K., et al. (2018). Trajectories of the Earth system in the anthropocene. *Proceedings of the National Academy of Sciences,* 115 (33): 8252–8259. https://doi.org/10.1073/pnas.1810141115.

Steger, M. B. (2013). *Globalization: A Very Short Introduction.* New York, NY: Oxford University Press.

Stiglitz, J. E. (2019). *People, Power, and Profits: Progressive Capitalism for an Age of Discontent.* New York, NY: W. W. Norton.

Streeck, W. (2016). *How Will Capitalism End? Essays on a Failing System.* London: Verso.

Taylor, K. (1999). Rapid climate change. *American Scientist* 87: 320–327.

Traub, J. (2018). Kofi Annan's tragic idealism. *New York Times*, August 20.

Trigger, B. G. (2003). *Understanding Early Civilizations: A Comparative Study.* Cambridge: Cambridge University Press.

United Nations. (1987). *Report of the World Commission on Environment and Development* (Bruntdland report). https://digitallibrary.un.org/record/139811.

United Nations. (2022). *The Sustainable Development Goals Report 2022.* https://unstats.un.org/sdgs/report/2022/.

Van Vugt, M. & Ahuja, A. (2011). *Naturally Selected: The Evolutionary Science of Leadership.* New York, NY: HarperCollins.

Wallace-Wells, D. (2019). *The Uninhabitable Earth: Life After Warming.* New York, NY: Tim Duggan Books.

Ward, D. R. (2002). *Water Wars: Drought, Flood, Folly, and the Politics of Thirst.* New York, NY: Penguin Group.

Wilson, E. O. (2012). *The Social Conquest of Earth.* New York, NY: Liveright Publishing.

Wilson, E .O. (2016). *Half Earth: Our Planet's Fight for Life.* New York, NY: Liveright Publishing.

Wood, M. C. (2014). *Nature's Trust: Environmental Law for a New Ecological Age.* New York, NY: Cambridge University Press.

World Bank. (2022a). *Poverty and Shared Prosperity.* Washington, DC: World Bank.

World Bank. (2022b). Climate migration deepening our solutions [blog], March 22.

World Bank. (n.d.). Water. www.worldbank.org/en/topic/water/overview.

World Resources Institute. (2019). *World Resources Report: Creating a Sustainable Food Future.* Washington, DC: World Resources Institute. http://research.wri.org/wrr-food.

Wray, L. R., Dantas, F., Fullwiler, S., Tcherneva, P. R., & Kelton, S. A. (2018). *Public Service Employment: A Path to Full Employment.* Annandale-on-Hudson, NY: Levy Economics Institute of Bard College.

Yunus, M. (2017). *A World of Three Zeros: The New Economics of Zero Poverty, Zero Unemployment, and Zero Net Carbon Emissions.* New York, NY: Perseus Books.

Zucman, G. (2015). *The Hidden Wealth of Nations: The Scourge of Tax Havens.* Chicago, IL: University of Chicago Press.

Cambridge Elements ☰

Applied Evolutionary Science

David F. Bjorklund
Florida Atlantic University

David F. Bjorklund is a Professor of Psychology at Florida Atlantic University in Boca
Raton, Florida. He is the Editor-in-Chief of the *Journal of Experimental Child Psychology*, the
Vice President of the Evolution Institute, and has written numerous articles and books on
evolutionary developmental psychology, with a particular interest in the role of
immaturity in evolution and development.

About the Series
This series presents original, concise, and authoritative reviews of key topics in applied
evolutionary science. Highlighting how an evolutionary approach can be applied to
real-world social issues, many Elements in this series will include findings from programs
that have produced positive educational, social, economic, or behavioral benefits.
Cambridge Elements in Applied Evolutionary Science is published in association
with the Evolution Institute.

 THE EVOLUTION INSTITUTE

Cambridge Elements ☰

Applied Evolutionary Science

Elements in the Series

Improving Breastfeeding Rates: Evolutionary Anthropological Insights for Public Health
Emily H. Emmott

The Hidden Talents Framework: Implications for Science, Policy, and Practice
Bruce J. Ellis, Laura S. Abrams, Ann S. Masten, Robert J. Sternberg, Nim Tottenham and Willem E. Frankenhuis

An Introduction to Positive Evolutionary Psychology
Glenn Geher, Megan Fritche, Avrey Goodwine, Julia Lombard, Kaitlyn Longo and Darcy Montana

Superorganism: Toward a New Social Contract for Our Endangered Species
Peter A. Corning

A full series listing is available at: www.cambridge.org/EAES

Printed in the United States
by Baker & Taylor Publisher Services